TEACHER'S PET PUBLICATIONS

LITPLAN TEACHER PACK
for
The View from Saturday
based on the book by
E. L. Konigsburg

Written by
Catherine Caldwell

© 2006 Teacher's Pet Publications
All Rights Reserved

This **LitPlan** for

The View from Saturday
has been brought to you by Teacher's Pet Publications, Inc.

Copyright Teacher's Pet Publications 2006
11504 Hammock Point
Berlin MD 21811

Only the student materials in this unit plan (such as worksheets, study questions, and tests) may be reproduced multiple times for use in the purchaser's classroom.

For any additional copyright questions,
contact Teacher's Pet Publications.

www.tpet.com

TABLE OF CONTENTS - *The View from Saturday*

Introduction	5
Unit Objectives	7
Reading Assignment Sheet	8
Unit Outline	9
Study Questions (Short Answer)	13
Quiz/Study Questions (Multiple Choice)	25
Pre-reading Vocabulary Worksheets	49
Lesson One (Introductory Lesson)	69
Nonfiction Assignment Sheet	74
Oral Reading Evaluation Form	76
Writing Assignment 1	85
Writing Assignment 2	95
Writing Assignment 3	109
Writing Evaluation Form	110
Vocabulary Review Activities	103
Extra Writing Assignments/Discussion ?s	97
Unit Review Activities	111
Unit Tests	115
Unit Resource Materials	153
Vocabulary Resource Materials	177

A FEW NOTES ABOUT THE AUTHOR
E. L. Konigsburg

"I knew I had been right about the spirit of adventure shared by good readers. I owe children a good story."

-Elaine Lobl Konigsburg

Elaine Lobl was born on February 20, 1930 in New York City. Early in her childhood, her family moved to small-town Pennsylvania, where Elaine graduated first in her high school class and became the first person from her family to attend college. The young woman earned a degree in chemistry from Carnegie Mellon, though graduate work at the University of Pittsburgh convinced her that she did not have the heart for further pursuit of the science. After she and her husband married, they moved to Florida, and Konigsburg began teaching science at a girls' school.

Through teaching young women, Konigsburg realized that she was more fascinated by the students she taught than the subject matter she presented. She left the classroom after a short time in order to raise her three children–Paul, Laurie, and Ross-- but continued to marvel at young people and their experiences in the world. While she was home raising her children, Konigsburg began taking art classes, as well. She discovered a natural talent for art, and several of her novels feature her original illustrations. Konigsburg's first novel *Jennifer, Hecate, Macbeth, William McKinley, and me, Elizabeth* won Newbery Honors in 1967, and it was followed by *From the Mixed-Up Files of Mrs. Basil E. Frankweiler*, which won the Newbery Medal in 1968. Over the next thirty years, Konigsburg would write over fifteen novels, including *The View from Saturday*, which earned her a second Newbery Medal in 1997.

INTRODUCTION

This LitPlan has been designed to develop students' reading, writing, thinking, and language skills through exercises and activities related to *The View from Saturday*. It includes 22 lessons, supported by extra resource materials.

The **introductory lesson** introduces students to the process of group collaboration and individual contribution as students participate in an "Information Scavenger Hunt" in the school library. Following the introductory activity, students are given a transition to explain how the activity relates to the book they are about to read. Students also are given the materials they will be using during the unit. The class will have an opportunity to draw conclusions about the novel based on a cursory examination of the cover and table of contents.

The **reading assignments** are approximately thirty pages each; some are a little shorter while others are a little longer. Students have approximately 15 minutes of pre-reading work to do prior to each reading assignment. This pre-reading work involves reviewing the study questions for the assignment and doing some vocabulary work for 6 to 12 vocabulary words they will encounter in their reading.

The **study guide questions** are fact-based questions; students can find the answers to these questions right in the text. These questions come in two formats: short answer or multiple choice. The best use of these materials is probably to use the short answer version of the questions as study guides for students (since answers will be more complete), and to use the multiple choice version for occasional quizzes.

The **vocabulary work** is intended to enrich students' vocabularies as well as to aid in the students' understanding of the book. Prior to each reading assignment, students will complete a two-part worksheet for approximately 6 to 12 vocabulary words in the upcoming reading assignment. Part I focuses on students' use of general knowledge and contextual clues by giving the sentence in which the word appears in the text. Students are then to write down what they think the words mean based on the words' usage. Part II nails down the definitions of the words by giving students dictionary definitions of the words and having students match the words to the correct definitions based on the words' contextual usage. Students should then have an understanding of the words when they meet them in the text.

After each reading assignment, students will go back and formulate answers for the study guide questions. Discussion of these questions serves as a **review** of the most important events and ideas presented in the reading assignments.

After students complete reading the work, there is a **vocabulary review** lesson which pulls together all of the fragmented vocabulary lists for the reading assignments and gives students a review of all of the words they have studied.

Following the vocabulary review, a lesson is devoted to the **extra discussion questions/writing assignments**. These questions focus on interpretation, critical analysis and personal response, employing a variety of thinking skills and adding to the students' understanding of the novel.

There is a **group theme project** in this unit. Students will divide into groups or 4 or 5 students based upon a common investigative interest. Each group will research a particular hobby, skill, subject or issue they would like to explore, thereby becoming the class experts on that topic. Each group will then develop an original product based on their study. A presentation day is scheduled in the unit so that students may benefit from one another's work, in addition to practicing their public speaking skills.

There are three **writing assignments** in this unit, each with the purpose of informing, persuading, or having students express personal opinions. The first writing assignment calls upon students to write a thank-you letter to someone who has bestowed kindness on them. The second writing assignment asks students to compose a narrative essay recalling a positive experience they have shared with a parent or grandparent. The third writing assignment allows students to express their own opinion regarding the "decline of Western Civilization," and charges them to write a speech that will persuade their classmates to take action in order to change that downward course.

There is a **nonfiction reading assignment**. Students must read nonfiction articles, books, etc. to gather information about their themes in our world today.

The **review lesson** pulls together all of the aspects of the unit. The teacher is given four or five choices of activities or games to use which all serve the same basic function of reviewing all of the information presented in the unit.

The **unit test** comes in two formats: multiple choice or short answer. As a convenience, two different tests for each format have been included. There is also an advanced short answer unit test for advanced students.

There are additional **support materials** included with this unit. The **Unit Resource Materials** section includes suggestions for an in-class library, crossword and word search puzzles related to the novel, and extra worksheets. There is a list of **bulletin board ideas** which gives the teacher suggestions for bulletin boards to go along with this unit. In addition, there is a list of **extra class activities** the teacher could choose from to enhance the unit or as a substitution for an exercise the teacher might feel is inappropriate for his/her class. **Answer keys** are located directly after the **reproducible student materials** throughout the unit. The **Vocabulary Resource Materials** section includes similar worksheets and games to reinforce the vocabulary words.

The **level** of this unit can be varied depending upon the criteria on which the individual assignments are graded, the teacher's expectations of his/her students in class discussions, and the formats chosen for the study guides, quizzes and test. If teachers have other ideas/activities they wish to use, they can usually easily be inserted prior to the review lesson.

UNIT OBJECTIVES - *The View from Saturday*

1. Through reading E. L. Konigsburg's *The View from Saturday*, students will explore themes of the novel and make connections to themselves and the larger world.

2. Students will demonstrate their understanding of the text on four levels: factual, interpretive, critical and personal.

3. Students will gain a better knowledge of nonfiction topics presented in the novel. Students will pursue their own interests within a larger group dynamic.

4. Students will be given the opportunity to practice reading aloud and silently to improve their skills in each area.

7. Students will answer questions to demonstrate their knowledge and understanding of the main events and characters in *The View from Saturday* as they relate to the author's theme development.

8. Students will enrich their vocabularies and improve their understanding of the novel through the vocabulary lessons prepared for use in conjunction with the novel.

9. The writing assignments in this unit are geared to several purposes:
    a. To have students demonstrate their abilities to inform, to persuade, or to express their own personal ideas
        Note: Students will demonstrate ability to write effectively to <u>inform</u> by developing and organizing facts to convey information. Students will demonstrate the ability to write effectively to <u>persuade</u> by selecting and organizing relevant information, establishing an argumentative purpose, and by designing an appropriate strategy for an identified audience. Students will demonstrate the ability to write effectively to <u>express personal ideas</u> by selecting a form and its appropriate elements.
    b. To check the students' reading comprehension
    c. To make students think about the ideas presented by the novel
    d. To encourage logical thinking
    e. To provide an opportunity to practice good grammar and improve students' use of the English language.

10. Students will read aloud, report, and participate in large and small group discussions to improve their public speaking and personal interaction skills.

READING ASSIGNMENT SHEET - *The View from Saturday*

Date Assigned	Chapters Assigned	Completion Date
	Chapter 1	
	Chapter 2	
	Chapter 3, Part 1	
	Chapter 3, Part 2	
	Chapters 4-6	
	Chapter 7	
	Chapters 8-12	

UNIT OUTLINE - *The View from Saturday*

1 Introduction	2 PVR Chapter 1 Oral Reading	3 Study? Chapter 1 Group Project	4 PVR Chapter 2, Part 1	5 Study? Chapter 2, Part 1 PVR Chapter 2, Part 2
6 Study? Chapter 2, Part 2 PVR Chapter 3, Part 1	7 P-Chapter 3, Part 2 Group Work	8 VR Chapter 3, Part 2	9 Writting Assignment 1	10 Study? Chapter 3, Part 2 PVR Chapters 4-6
11 Study? Chapters 4-6 PVR Chapter 7	12 Study? Chapter 7 Class Activity	13 PVR Chapters 8-12	14 Study? Chapters 8-12 Class Activity	15 Writing Assignment 2
16 Extra Writing/Discussion Questions	17 Vocabulary Review	18 Group Presentations	19 Lesson: Allusions	20 Writing Assignment #3
21 Unit Review	22 Test	23	24	25

Key: P = Preview Study Questions   V = Vocabulary Work   R = Read

STUDY GUIDE QUESTIONS

SHORT ANSWER STUDY GUIDE QUESTIONS - *The View from Saturday*

Chapter 1
1. Who selects the team for the Academic Bowl?
2. How does she usually explain her selection?
3. What do the team members call themselves?
4. What is "extraordinary" about The Souls?
5. What is the name of The Souls' school?
6. Which two schools remain on Bowl Day?
7. In what city is Bowl Day held?
8. Who is the "first chosen" to answer a question on Bowl Day? What is the subject of the first question?

Noah Writes a B & B Letter
1. What is a B & B letter?
2. To whom must Noah write a B & B letter?
3. What items does Noah remove from his desk to begin writing?
4. What items does Noah place on his list of things to include in his B & B letter?
5. What is Century Village?
6. Who gets married at Century Village?
7. Who organizes the wedding?
8. Who teaches Noah calligraphy? Why?
9. Why is Noah in great demand on the day of the wedding?
10. Who is supposed to be the best man? Why doesn't he fulfil his role?
11. Who is actually best man at Izzy's wedding?
12. What are the "specially-marked invitations?" What gifts are offered?

Chapter 2
1. Who is Dr. Roy Clayton Rohmer?
2. Who is standing at the podium?
3. Briefly describe the appearance of the man at the podium.
4. What do Dr. Rohmer and Mrs. Olinski discuss after The Souls win the Epiphany Middle School Championship?

Nadia Tells of Turtle Love
1. What reason does Nadia's mother give for moving back to New York?
2. What month does Nadia spend with her father in Florida?
3. How does Nadia describe Margaret's appearance?
4. What does Nadia claim is her father's "new best thing?"
5. Where did Margaret live before moving to Florida?
6. What is Nadia's mother's profession? For whom does she work?
7. Who comes to visit Margaret in Florida?
8. What brings Margaret and Izzy together?
9. For how many months do the turtle patrols monitor the nests?

The View From Saturday Short Answer Study Questions Page 2

10. What designation do loggerheads have according to the Department of Environmental Protection?
11. Why does Nadia call herself a mixed breed?
12. What are "permitted volunteers?"
13. What time of day do turtles generally hatch? Why do they sometimes need a little help making it to the ocean?
14. What "bombshell" does Nadia's father drop after seeing *Phantom of the Opera*?
15. What information does Ethan give Nadia about her mother's job?
16. How does Nadia react to Ethan's disclosing the things he knows about her life?
17. Why does Grandpa place a midnight phone call to Nadia and her father?

Chapter 3
1. Who was principal of Mrs. Olinski's school the first year that she taught?
2. Why did Mrs. Olinski leave teaching?
3. Why didn't Mrs. Olinski tell Ethan that she knew his grandmother?
4. Who knows the answer to the Women in American History question?
5. What does Ethan consider the worst part of the school day?
6. What is Ethan's strategy as he sits on the bus the first day?
7. Why does Ethan hope his teacher is new to Epiphany?
8. How does Ethan describe his older brother Lucas?
9. Who does Ethan's mother refer to as "them?"
10. How does Ethan define the difference between farmers and suburbanites?
11. Describe the pair of individuals standing in front of Sillington House.
12. What are the Singhs' plans for Sillington house? What was Julian's father's former occupation?
13. What unusual physical characteristic does Mrs. Olinski discuss with her class on the first day of school?
14. What physical characteristic does Ethan most admire about Nadia?
15. Who does Mrs. Olinski find alone in the classroom after lunch the first day of school?
16. What does Ham Knapp take from Julian after he gets off the bus? What does he do with it? What is Julian's response?
17. What are Ethan's dreams for the future?
18. What does Julian give Ethan with the payment for the pumpkins?
19. What gift does Ethan take to the tea party? Nadia? Noah?
20. What skill does Julian display as the group looks for the last piece of the jigsaw puzzle?
21. What do the four sixth-graders come to be called? Who gives them their name?

The View From Saturday Short Answer Study Questions Page 3

Chapter 4
1. What possible challenge does Mrs. Olinski decide to examine after lunch?
2. What object does Julian show to The Souls at their weekly tea?
3. What project–other than stripping wallpaper–do The Souls undertake?

Julian Narrates When Ginger Played Annie's Sandy
1. What do Noah and Nadia bicker about at the Thanksgiving Saturday tea?
2. What is Nadia's dog's name?
3. What important trick does Julian teach The Souls in order to train Ginger?
4. Whose dog does Ginger compete against for the part of Sandy? Does Ginger get the part?
5. Whose presence at rehearsal is Julian concerned about? Why?
6. Who are the first paying guests at Sillington House?
7. What does Julian overhear Ham Knapp discussing during the ride to the matinee?
8. What is Ham's mother's profession?
9. How does Julian secretly communicate with The Souls at the matinee?
10. What news does Nadia tell Julian about Ginger's performance?
11. What dilemma is Julian faced with regarding the dog treats?
12. Why does Mrs. Reynolds become upset with the audience?
13. Why does Mrs. Olinski call Julian aside following the performance?
14. How does Julian resolve his dilemma over the doggie treats?

Chapter 5
1. How did Mrs. Olinski select her academic bowl team? How did this differ from other teachers' methods?
2. Between which two individuals did Mrs. Olinski choose the fourth member of her team?
3. Why was she reluctant to choose Julian?
4. Who pushes Mrs. Olinski's wheelchair to the entrance to Sillington House?
5. What does Mrs. Olinski observe about the four sixth graders at Sillington House that she considers unusual?
6. What two realizations does Mrs. Olinski make at the close of chapter 5?

Chapter 6
1. Who wins the competition between Epiphany's sixth grade and seventh grade teams?
2. Which grade do the seventh graders decide to support?
3. Who wins the competition against the eighth graders?

The View From Saturday Short Answer Study Questions Page 4

Chapter 7
1. How does the team respond to Julian's defiance of the commissioner?
2. What action does the commissioner take?
3. Who is Mr. LeDue?
4. What is Dr. Rohmer's state of mind before the competition?
5. List the things Dr. Rohmer is concerned about before the competition.
6. Who is Mr. Homer Fairbain?
7. Why does Dr. Rohmer feel the competition will draw a large audience?
8. How do the sixth graders react when Epiphany beats Knightsbridge?

Chapter 8
1. How many regions are in the state? How are they named?
2. Why do The Souls decline a Saturday practice at the school?
3. What is Mrs. Olinski's response to the Souls' declining the Saturday practice?
4. Who greets Mrs. Olinski at her van when she arrives at Sillington House?
5. How does Mr. Singh make Mrs. Olinski uneasy?
6. What was unusual about the question cards that Mr. Singh places in front of Mrs. Olinski?

Chapter 9
1. Why does the commissioner of education penalize Julian?
2. What does the panel discover and tell the commissioner?
3. Why does Dr. Rohmer call a press conference?
4. How is transportation provided for the Epiphany townsfolk to go to Albany?

Chapter 10
1. Who rides with Mrs. Olinski to the competition in Albany?
2. What is the final question of the competition?
3. Which team member answers the final question of the competition in Albany correctly?
4. Which team wins the competition in Albany?
5. What is the trophy called?

Chapter 11
1. Who does Mrs. Olinski ask for an explanation regarding her choices for the quiz bowl team?
2. What is Mr. Singh's explanation of Mrs. Olinski's member choices for the bowl team?
3. What have all of The Souls found?
4. Which two books does Mrs. Olinski look at just before going to bed after Bowl Day?

Chapter 12
1. Who opens the door to Sillington House when Mrs. Olinski arrives?
2. What question does Mrs. Olinski ask The Souls when they are seated at their final meeting at Sillington House? What is their response?

ANSWER KEY SHORT ANSWER STUDY GUIDE QUESTIONS - *The View from Saturday*

Chapter 1

1. Who selects the team for the Academic Bowl?
   Mrs. Eva Marie Olinski selects her team for the Bowl from her class of sixth graders.
2. How does she usually explain her selection?
   She usually says that the "four members of her team had skills that balanced one another."
3. What do the team members call themselves?
   The team members call themselves The Souls.
4. What is "extraordinary" about The Souls?
   Although they were all sixth graders, they were able make it to the state championship academic bowl.
5. What is the name of The Souls' school?
   The Souls attend Epiphany Middle School.
6. Which two schools remain on Bowl Day?
   Epiphany and Maxwell compete on Bowl Day.
7. In what city is Bowl Day held?
   Bowl Day takes place in Albany.
8. Who is the "first chosen" to answer a question on Bowl Day? What is the subject of the first question?
   Noah Gershom answers first. The question is about calligraphy.

Noah Writes a B & B Letter

1. What is a B & B letter?
   A B & B letter is a "bread and butter" letter written to thank a host or hostess for allowing one to stay as a houseguest.
2. To whom must Noah write a B & B letter? Why?
   Noah must write a B & B letter to his Grandma and Grandpa for allowing him to stay with them while his mother went on a cruise with his father.
3. What items does Noah remove from his desk to begin writing?
   Noah gets out notepaper, ballpoint pen (which he returns to the drawer), calligraphy pen, ink, sharpened pencil, and a pad of Post-it notes.
4. What items does Noah place on his list of things to include in his B & B letter?
   He lists red wagon, tuxedo shirt, calligraphy pen and bottle of ink, and Post-it notes.
5. What is Century Village?
   Century Village is a retirement community in Florida.
6. Who gets married at Century Village?
   Margaret Draper and Izzy Diamondstein
7. Who organizes the wedding?
   The residents of Century Village all contribute their time, money, and talents.
8. Who teaches Noah calligraphy? Why?
   Tillie Nachman, a resident of Century Village, teaches Noah calligraphy because he helps address the invitations to the wedding in calligraphy.

9. Why is Noah in great demand on the day of the wedding?
   Noah was needed to take things to the clubhouse in his red wagon.
10. Who is supposed to be the best man? Why doesn't he fulfil his role?
    Izzy's son Allen Diamondstein is supposed to be the best man, but he falls over the handle to the red wagon and hurt his ankle.
11. Who is actually the best man at Izzy's wedding?
    Noah is the best man.
12. What are the "specially-marked invitations?" What gifts are offered?
    They were the invitations marked with the paw print of Tillie's cat, T.S., which was masked by a post-it note announcing it was a specially marked invitation. Gifts included the hand-painted T-shirt (with fabric painting lessons), calligraphy pen and ink (with calligraphy lessons), post-it notes (with an orchid donated in return), the red wagon (given back to the village) and the opportunity to give up the gift.

Chapter 2
1. Who is Dr. Roy Clayton Rohmer?
   He is the District Superintendent of Clarion County.
2. Who is standing at the podium?
   The commissioner of education is standing at the podium, "king for a day."
3. Briefly describe the appearance of the man at the podium.
   He wears a "precision fit pin-striped suit and a white-on-dazzling-white shirt...He was dressed, brushed, coiffed, and blow-dried not just to be seen but to be looked at."
4. What do Dr. Rohmer and Mrs. Olinski discuss after The Souls win the Epiphany Middle School Championship?
   They discuss the concepts of multiculturalism and diversity, although Mrs. Olinski speaks mostly tongue-in-cheek, while Dr. Rohmer speaks with the utmost ironic reverence.

Nadia Tells of Turtle Love
1. What reason does Nadia's mother give for moving back to New York?
   She claims to need some autumn in her life.
2. What month does Nadia spend with her father in Florida?
   Nadia spends August with her father.
3. How does Nadia describe Margaret's appearance?
   She is a "short blonde" who "dresses atrociously." She likens her to a Granny Smith Apple.
4. What does Nadia claim is her father's "new best thing?"
   Nadia claims her father's "new best thing" is hovering.
5. Where did Margaret live before moving to Florida?
   She lived in Epiphany, New York.
6. What is Nadia's mother's profession? For whom does she work?
   She is a dental hygienist who works for Dr. Gershom, Noah's father.
7. Who comes to visit Margaret in Florida?
   Margaret's grandson Ethan Potter comes to visit.

8. What brings Margaret and Izzy together?
    Turtles brought them together.
9. For how many months do the turtle patrols monitor the nests?
    Patrols monitor the nests from May-October (6 months).
10. What designation do loggerheads have according to the Department of Environmental Protection?
    They are a threatened species.
11. Why does Nadia call herself a mixed breed?
    She is half-Jewish and half-Protestant.
12. What are "permitted volunteers?"
    Permitted volunteers are licensed to either move or dig out a nest after the eggs have hatched. They must be supervised by a more experienced individual, however, such as Margaret.
13. What time of day do turtles generally hatch? Why do they sometimes need a little help making it to the ocean?
    Turtles generally hatch at night, so they might be disoriented by the lights of civilization on the shore and begin to head away from the ocean, rather than toward it.
14. What "bombshell" does Nadia's father drop after seeing *Phantom of the Opera*?
    He asks Margaret to be listed on her permit.
15. What information does Ethan give Nadia about her mother's job?
    Ethan knew that his grandmother Margaret set up Nadia's mother's job interview with Dr. Gershom, but Nadia had known nothing about it.
16. How does Nadia react to Ethan's disclosing the things he knew about her life?
    She is furious that Ethan knows so much about her life that she doesn't.
17. Why does Grandpa place a midnight phone call to Nadia and her father?
    A noreaster is on its way that threatens the turtle nest. He needs their help to harvest the hatchlings so they will not be swept ashore.

Chapter 3
1. Who was principal of Mrs. Olinski's school the first year that she taught?
    Margaret Draper was the principal.
2. Why did Mrs. Olinski leave teaching?
    She was in an auto accident that left her a widow and a paraplegic.
3. Why didn't Mrs. Olinski tell Ethan that she knew his grandmother?
    She wanted "to discover Ethan all by herself."
4. Who knows the answer to the women in American history question?
    Ethan Potter knows the answer.
5. What does Ethan consider the worst part of the school day?
    Ethan considers the bus ride the worst part of the school day.
6. What is Ethan's strategy as he sits on the bus the first day?
    He attempts to take up the entire seat with his body and his backpack so that he will be able to have the seat to himself for the remainder of the year.
7. Why does Ethan hope his teacher is new to Epiphany?
    A new teacher would not know that he was the younger brother of Lucas Potter.

8. How does Ethan describe his older brother Lucas?
    "There is nothing wrong with Lucas, and that is what is wrong with him." He is a star in everything he does, and everyone in town is aware of his multifaceted genius.
9. Who does Ethan's mother refer to as "them?"
    She calls residents of The Farm subdivision "*them*."
10. How does Ethan define the difference between farmers and suburbanites?
    "To *them* [suburbanites] *farming is a lifestyle not a livelihood.*"
11. Describe the pair of individuals standing in front of Sillington House.
    A man in a long blue apron and white turban stands beside a boy wearing shorts and knee socks.
12. What are the Singhs' plans for Sillington house? What is Julian's father's former occupation?
    They plan to turn it into a bed and breakfast inn. Mr. Singh was formerly a chef on the cruise ship *Skylark*.
13. What unusual physical characteristic does Mrs. Olinski discuss with her class on the first day of school?
    She discusses her paraplegia.
14. What physical characteristic does Ethan most admire about Nadia?
    He admires the way the fringes of her hair frame her face in a halo.
15. Who does Mrs. Olinski find alone in the classroom after lunch the first day of school?
    She finds Julian Singh.
16. What does Ham Knapp take from Julian after he gets off the bus? What does he do with it? What is Julian's response?
    Ham takes Julian's book bag and uses a black felt tip pen to inscribe "I am a ass." Julian responds by returning the next day with the phrase transformed into the phrase "I am a passenger on spaceship earth." A faint halo encircled the original sentence, as though Julian had made an attempt to erase Ham's words.
17. What are Ethan's dreams for the future?
    He wants to design costumes or stage sets for the theater.
18. What does Julian give Ethan with the payment for the pumpkins?
    A post-it note with the phrase *"Alice's Adventures in Wonderland* Chapter VII Title" is tucked inside the bill.
19. What gift does Ethan take to the tea party? Nadia? Noah?
    Ethan takes a jigsaw puzzle, Nadia takes one of Ginger's puppies, and Noah takes a calligraphy pen, ink, pad, and instruction book.
20. What skill does Julian display as the group looks for the last piece of the jigsaw puzzle?
    He shows his ability to perform slight-of-hand magic tricks.
21. What do the four sixth-graders come to be called? Who gives them their name?
    They are called The Souls. Nadia wins the honor of naming the group because she pulls off the longest piece of unbroken wallpaper when the group strips a room of Sillington House.

Chapter 4

1. What possible challenge does Mrs. Olinski decide to examine in her classroom after lunch?
    She wanted to be sure that all of her students would be able to see what she wrote on the board since she could only reach so high from her wheelchair.
2. What object does Julian show to The Souls at their weekly tea?
    He shows an ivory monkey that is capable of balancing on one of its four limbs.
3. What project–other than stripping wallpaper–do The Souls undertake?
    They want to help Mrs. Olinski "stand on her own two feet."

Julian Narrates When Ginger Played Annie's Sandy

1. What do Noah and Nadia bicker about at the Thanksgiving Saturday tea?
    They bicker about whether or not Ginger would be an appropriate choice to play Sandy in the high school production of *Annie*.
2. What is Nadia's dog's name?
    Ginger is her dog's name.
3. What important trick does Julian teach The Souls in order to train Ginger?
    He teaches them to palm doggy biscuits without making Ginger salivate.
4. Whose dog does Ginger compete against for the part of Sandy? Does Ginger get the part?
    Michael Froelich's dog Arnold competes against Ginger. Ginger gets the part of Sandy.
5. Whose presence at rehearsal is Julian concerned about? Why?
    He does not like the fact that Michael Froelich will be attending rehearsals (since Arnold is Ginger's understudy). Michael is one of Hamilton Knapp's cohorts, and he worries that Michael will bring harm to Ginger or that he may be harboring malicious intent.
6. Who are the first paying guests at Sillington House?
    Margaret and Izzy Diamondstein are the first paying guests.
7. What does Julian overhear Ham Knapp discussing during the ride to the matinee?
    Julian hears Ham talking about the doggie treats he has laced with tranquilizers and laxatives and his plans to give these to Nadia for Ginger in order to cause Ginger to embarrass herself and pass out.
8. What is Ham's mother's profession?
    She is a veterinarian.
9. How does Julian secretly communicate with The Souls at the matinee?
    He places a Year-of-the-Souls penny in their palms, which signals to them that he needs to communicate with them.
10. What news does Nadia tell Julian about Ginger's performance?
    Froelich's dog Arnold will be playing the part of Sandy during the matinee since Froelich and Arnold have attended rehearsals so faithfully.
11. What dilemma is Julian faced with?
    Julian must decide whether to allow Arnold to consume the doggie treats that Ham has doctored.
12. Why does Mrs. Reynolds become upset with the audience?
    The audience, led by Ham, has caused a great deal of inappropriate ruckus.

13. Why does Mrs. Olinski call Julian aside following the performance?
    She wants Julian to ride to Sillington House in her van so that she can visit with Margaret and Izzy.
14. How does Julian resolve his dilemma over the doggie treats?
    He removes Ham's treats from harm's way, and he substitutes Ginger's safe treats. He then uses his "chops" to drop the laced treats into Ham's lap while he is sitting beside his mother in the veterinary van.

Chapter 5
1. How does Mrs. Olinski select her academic bowl team? How does this differ from other teachers' methods?
    She appoints them, rather than having them try out.
2. Which two individuals does Mrs. Olinski choose between to become the fourth member of her team?
    She wavers between Ham Knapp and Julian Singh.
3. Why is she reluctant to choose Julian?
    She feels that he is a loner, not a team player, whereas Ham Knapp, on the other hand, has a great many friends.
4. Who pushes Mrs. Olinski's wheelchair to the entrance to Sillington House?
    Julian's father pushes her wheelchair.
5. What unusual thing does Mrs. Olinski observe about the four sixth graders at Sillington House?
    The children talk to each other courteously, taking turns, and listening to one another and enjoying one another's company.
6. What two realizations does Mrs. Olinski make at the close of chapter 5?
    She realizes that Julian Singh will be the fourth member of the quiz bowl team, and she knows she will drink tea again at Sillington House.

Chapter 6
1. Who wins the competition between Epiphany's sixth grade and seventh grade teams?
    The sixth graders win.
2. Which grade do the seventh graders decide to support?
    They decide to support the sixth graders.
3. Who wins the competition against the eighth graders?
    The sixth graders win.

Chapter 7
1. How does the team respond to Julian's defiance of the commissioner?
    They clearly, though quietly, support him.
2. What action does the commissioner take?
    He takes no action; he is speechless.
3. Who is Mr. LeDue?
    Mr. LeDue is the principal of Knightsbridge Middle School.

4. What is Dr. Rohmer's state of mind before the competition?
   He is worried.
5. List the things Dr. Rohmer is concerned about before the competition.
   He is concerned about his contract renewal, he is concerned about the district playoffs, and he is concerned about how Fairbain's performance might affect his other two concerns.
6. Who is Mr. Homer Fairbain?
   Fairbain is the deputy superintendent in charge of instruction who acts as master of ceremonies for the district play-offs.
7. Why does Dr. Rohmer feel the competition will draw a large audience?
   He thinks so "partly because people were curious about having a sixth grade team be a contender for the district middle school champion ship but mostly because everyone would be waiting for Homer Fairbain to goof."
8. How do the sixth graders react when Epiphany beats Knightsbridge?
   They take a piece of rope from their pockets silently, and they pin it on their shirts as if it is a medal.

Chapter 8
1. How many regions are in the state? How are they named?
   The eight regions are named for major bodies of water that touch the counties.
2. Why do The Souls decline a Saturday practice at the school?
   They already have plans to meet for tea at Sillington House.
3. What is Mrs. Olinski's response to The Souls' declining the Saturday practice?
   She is a bit surprised, but then she decides she will join them for tea.
4. Who greets Mrs. Olinski at her van when she arrives at Sillington House?
   Mr. Singh greets her.
5. How does Mr. Singh make Mrs. Olinski uneasy?
   He talks to her about the fact that she almost chose Ham Knapp for the team. He even calls Ham by name, even though Mrs. Olinski has never told anyone about her indecision over the fourth member of the team.
6. What is unusual about the question cards that Mr. Singh places in front of Mrs. Olinski?
   The questions are not only handwritten, but written in calligraphy.

Chapter 9
1. Why does the commissioner of education penalize Julian?
   He cites Julian for arguing with a ruling from the panel, and he takes away the two points Julian has just earned.
2. What does the panel discover and tell the commissioner?
   They discover that Julian was correct, and they show the evidence to the commissioner.
3. Why does Dr. Rohmer call a press conference?
   He wants the positive publicity that the press conference can bring to him.
4. How is transportation provided for the Epiphany townsfolk to go to Albany?
   After everyone at the Village watched the press conference on tape, Bella Dubinsky from Century Village designed T-shirts to sell to raise the money for buses.

Chapter 10
1. Who rides with Mrs. Olinski to the competition in Albany?
   Mr. Singh and Julian ride with Mrs. Olinski.
2. What is the final question of the competition?
   "What was the true name and occupation of the author of the work of fiction where we meet the original Humpty Dumpty?"
3. Which team member answers the final question of the competition in Albany correctly?
   Julian does.
4. Which team wins the Albany competition?
   Epiphany Middle School wins.
5. What is the trophy called?
   It is called a loving cup.

Chapter 11
1. Who does Mrs. Olinski ask for an explanation regarding her choices for the quiz bowl team?
   She asks Mr. Singh.
2. What is Mr. Singh's explanation of Mrs. Olinski's member choices for the bowl team?
   He explains that each of The Souls have returned from a journey: Noah (from Century Village), Nadia (from the Sargasso Sea), Ethan (from a ride on the school bus), and Julian (from his journey on the ship)
3. What have all of The Souls found?
   They have found kindness.
4. Which two books does Mrs. Olinski look at just before going to bed after Bowl Day?
   She looks at *Alice in Wonderland* and *Through the Looking Glass*.

Chapter 12
1. Who opens the door to Sillington House when Mrs. Olinski arrives?
   The Souls open it.
2. What question does Mrs. Olinski ask The Souls when they are seated at their final meeting at Sillington House? What is their response?
   She asks, "Did I choose you, or did you choose me?"
   They reply, "Yes!"

STUDY GUIDE/QUIZ QUESTIONS - *The View from Saturday*
Multiple Choice Format

Chapter 1
1. Who selects the team for the Academic Bowl?
   A. Mrs. Olinski
   B. Margaret Draper
   C. The principal
   D. The PTO president
2. How does she usually explain her selection?
   A. She chooses the students with the highest grades.
   B. She draws names at random.
   C. She accepts volunteers.
   D. She chooses students with skills that balance each other.
3. What do the team members call themselves?
   A. The Fabulous Four
   B. The Souls
   C. The Turtle Doves
   D. The Chops
4. What is "extraordinary" about The Souls?
   A. They are quadruplets.
   B. They speak 12 languages among them.
   C. They make it to the state championship as sixth graders.
   D. They are also champion racquetball players.
5. What is the name of The Souls' school?
   A. Knightsbridge Middle
   B. Maxwell Middle
   C. Epiphany Middle
   D. Loggerhead Middle
6. Which two schools remain on championship Bowl Day?
   A. Epiphany and Knightsbridge
   B. Epiphany and Maxwell
   C. Maxwell and Knightsbridge
   D. Maxwell and Loggerhead
7. In what city is Bowl Day held?
   A. Albany
   B. Chicago
   C. New York City
   D. Epiphany
8. What is the subject of the first question?
   A. New York history
   B. Mathematics
   C. Calligraphy
   D. Acronyms

The View From Saturday Multiple Choice Study/Quiz Questions Page 2

Noah Writes a B & B Letter
1. What is a B & B letter?
    A. A thank-you note
    B. A request for reservations at a bed and breakfast inn
    C. A note mailed on the bed and breakfast inn letterhead
    D. A note of apology
2. To whom must Noah write such a letter?
    A. Sillington House
    B. His grandparents at Century Village
    C. Allen Diamondstein
    D. Mrs. Olinski
3. What items does Noah use to write his B&B letter?
    A. Artist pencils
    B. A ballpoint pen
    C. Calligraphy materials
    D. A laptop computer
4. Which of the following items does Noah place on his list of things to include in his B & B letter?
    A. Red wagon and a tuxedo shirt
    B. A birthday cake and new swim suit
    C. A trip to Disneyworld
    D. The new laptop computer
5. What is Century Village?
    A. An historic town founded in south Florida in 1800
    B. A futuristic representation of the world in 2100
    C. A retirement community
    D. A shopping district
6. Who gets married at Century Village?
    A. The governor of Florida
    B. The owner of Century Village
    C. Noah's parents
    D. Margaret Draper and Izzy Diamondstein
7. Who organizes the wedding?
    A. A professional wedding consultant
    B. Noah's mother and father
    C. The sixth graders at Epiphany Middle School
    D. The residents of Century Village
8. Who teaches Noah calligraphy?
    A. Margaret Draper
    B. Julian Singh
    C. Tillie Nachman
    D. Izzy Diamondstein

The View From Saturday Multiple Choice Study/Quiz Questions Page 3

9. Why is Noah in great demand on the day of the wedding?
    A. He drives everyone in the golf cart.
    B. He ties everyone's bow ties.
    C. He hauls items in his red wagon.
    D. He keeps the groom calm.

10. Who is supposed to be the best man?
    A. Noah's father
    B. Allen Diamondstein
    C. Izzy Diamondstein
    D. Lucas Potter

11. Who is actually best man?
    A. Allen
    B. Noah
    C. Izzy
    D. Lucas

12. What are the "specially-marked invitations?"
    A. Invitations marked with a paw print and post-it note
    B. Invitations for guests who sit on the front row
    C. Invitations for the family members of the bride and groom
    D. Invitations for guests who wanted to be photographed

The View From Saturday Multiple Choice Study/Quiz Questions Page 4

Chapter 2
1. Who is Dr. Roy Clayton Rohmer?
    A. The dentist in Epiphany
    B. The veterinarian in Epiphany
    C. The Commissioner of Education
    D. The District Superintedent of Clarion County
2. Who is standing at the podium?
    A. Mrs. Olinski
    B. Noah
    C. The governor
    D. The commissioner
3. Briefly describe the appearance of the man at the podium.
    A. Dressed, coiffed and blow-dried
    B. Unclean and disheveled
    C. Tall and extremely thin
    D. Angry and red-faced
4. What do Dr. Rohmer and Mrs. Olinski discuss after The Souls win the Epiphany Middle School Championship?
    A. Transportation issues
    B. Mrs. Olinski's pay raise
    C. Multiculturalism and diversity
    D. The decline of Western Civilization

Nadia Tells of Turtle Love
1. What reason does Nadia's mother give for moving back to New York?
    A. She finds a job there.
    B. She misses the autumn.
    C. She cannot afford to live in Florida.
    D. Her family is in New York.
2. What month does Nadia spend with her father in Florida?
    A. June
    B. July
    C. August
    D. September
3. How does Nadia describe Margaret's appearance?
    A. She is a tall, slim brunette.
    B. She is a short blonde who dresses atrociously.
    C. She is a glamorous redhead.
    D. She doesn't comment on Margaret's appearance.

The View From Saturday Multiple Choice Study/Quiz Questions Page 5

4. What does Nadia claim is her father's "new best thing?"
    A. His laptop computer
    B. Hovering
    C. Turtle patrolling
    D. His new SUV
5. Where did Margaret live before moving to Florida?
    A. Epiphany, NY
    B. Washington, DC
    C. Charlottesville, VA
    D. Los Angeles, CA
6. What is Nadia's mother's profession?
    A. She is a dentist.
    B. She is a veterinarian.
    C. She is a dental hygienist.
    D. She is a teacher.
7. Who comes to visit Margaret in Florida?
    A. Mrs. Olinski
    B. Izzy
    C. Noah
    D. Ethan Potter
8. What brings Margaret and Izzy together?
    A. Allen
    B. Turtles
    C. Ballroom dance classes
    D. A mutual love for Zora Neale Hurston novels
9. For how many months do the turtle patrols monitor the nests?
    A. All year long
    B. 2 months
    C. 9 months
    D. 6 months
10. What designation do loggerheads have according to the Department of Environmental Protection?
    A. Extinct
    B. Endangered
    C. Threatened
    D. Thriving
11. Why does Nadia call herself a mixed breed?
    A. Because her pet is not pure-bred
    B. Because she likes both country and rock-and-roll music
    C. Because she loves winter and summer
    D. Because she is half-Jewish and half-Protestant

The View From Saturday Multiple Choice Study/Quiz Questions Page 6

12. What are "permitted volunteers?"
    A. Volunteers that have passed a test and can work at a hospital
    B. Volunteers that are licensed to move a turtle nest
    C. Volunteers that are licensed to drive the Book Mobile
    D. Volunteers that are licensed to become tutors in the schools
13. What time of day do turtles generally hatch?
    A. Morning
    B. Noon
    C. Afternoon
    D. Night
14. What "bombshell" does Nadia's father drop after seeing *Phantom of the Opera*?
    A. He is getting remarried.
    B. He is moving to New York.
    C. He wants to be listed on Margaret's turtle permit.
    D. He is quitting his job.
15. What information does Ethan give Nadia about her mother's job?
    A. Margaret set up the interview.
    B. Her mother is going to be fired.
    C. Her mother is getting a raise.
    D. Her mother is unhappy with her job.
16. How does Nadia react?
    A. She is grateful.
    B. She is angry.
    C. She is scared.
    D. She is indifferent.
17. Why does Grandpa place a midnight phone call to Nadia and her father?
    A. Because Margaret has had heart attack
    B. To wish them a happy New Year
    C. Because they did not arrive at his house on time
    D. To help rescue the turtles from the storm

The View From Saturday Multiple Choice Study/Quiz Questions Page 7

Chapter 3
1. Who was principal of Mrs. Olinski's school the first year that she taught?
    A. Dr. Rohmer
    B. The commissioner
    C. Margaret Draper
    D. Izzy Diamondstein
2. Why did Mrs. Olinski leave teaching?
    A. She was in a car accident.
    B. She wanted to pursue a different career.
    C. She gave birth to her first child.
    D. She moved to Europe.
3. Why doesn't Mrs. Olinski tell Ethan that she knew his grandmother?
    A. She is ashamed.
    B. She wants to discover Ethan for herself.
    C. She knows Ethan does not speak to his grandmother.
    D. She doesn't realize Ethan is Margaret's grandson.
4. Who knows the answer to the women in American history question?
    A. Maxwell
    B. Julian
    C. Nadia
    D. Ethan
5. What does Ethan consider the worst part of the school day?
    A. Homeroom
    B. The bus ride
    C. Lunch
    D. Math
6. What is Ethan's strategy as he sits on the bus the first day?
    A. Find someone to talk to
    B. Pretend to be asleep
    C. Take up the entire seat so he can have it alone all year
    D. Figure out a way to avoid riding the bus for the remainder of the year
7. Why does Ethan hope his teacher is new to Epiphany?
    A. He doesn't like any of the other teachers.
    B. He has gotten in a lot of trouble in the past.
    C. He doesn't want his teacher to compare him to his older brother.
    D. He is bored with school.
8. How does Ethan describe his older brother Lucas?
    A. He's "Angry and withdrawn."
    B. He's "Young and whiny."
    C. There's "nothing wrong with him, and that's what's wrong with him."
    D. He's "Completely forgettable."

The View From Saturday Multiple Choice Study/Quiz Questions Page 8

9. Who does Ethan's mother refer to as "*them*"?
    A. New York Mets
    B. Suburbanites
    C. Men
    D. Her parents
10. How does Ethan define the difference between farmers and suburbanites?
    A. Lifestyle v. livelihood
    B. John Deere v. Volvo
    C. Dirt v. asphalt
    D. Wood v. vinyl
11. Describe the pair of individuals standing in front of Sillington House.
    A. A woman in a wheelchair is sitting next to a man in a turban.
    B. A man in a long, blue apron and turban is standing next to a boy wearing shorts and knee socks.
    C. A boy wearing shorts and knee socks is standing next to a woman in a wheelchair.
    D. A man wearing shorts and knee socks is standing next to a boy carrying a large bag.
12. What are the Singhs' plans for Sillington house?
    A. Tear it down to build a new home
    B. Turn it into a bed and breakfast
    C. Turn it into an orphanage
    D. Turn it into a dentist office
13. What unusual physical characteristic does Mrs. Olinski discuss with her class on the first day of school?
    A. Albinoism
    B. Green hair
    C. Paraplegia
    D. Orange skin
14. What physical characteristic does Ethan most admire about Nadia?
    A. Eyes
    B. Hands
    C. Halo hair
    D. Legs
15. Who does Mrs. Olinski find alone in the classroom after lunch the first day of school?
    A. Ham Knapp
    B. Ethan
    C. Julian
    D. Ginger

The View From Saturday Multiple Choice Study/Quiz Questions Page 9

16. What does Ham Knapp take from Julian after he gets off the bus?
    A. His shoes
    B. His pencil
    C. His lunch
    D. His bookbag
17. What are Ethan's dreams for the future?
    A. To become costume/set designer
    B. To take over the family farm
    C. To become a dentist
    D. To go in business with Lucas
18. What does Julian give Ethan with the payment for the pumpkins?
    A. A Post-it note with a chapter title
    B. A book
    C. A movie
    D. A penny
19. What gift does Ethan take to the tea party?
    A. A book
    B. A cake
    C. A puzzle
    D. A pizza
20. What skill does Julian display as the group looks for the last piece of the jigsaw puzzle?
    A. Excellent sense of smell
    B. Slight-of-hand
    C. Singing talent
    D. Dancing ability
21. What do the four sixth-graders come to be called?
    A. The Four Tops
    B. The Quads
    C. Fire Team
    D. The Souls

The View From Saturday Multiple Choice Study/Quiz Questions Page 10

Chapter 4
1. What possible challenge does Mrs. Olinski decide to examine after lunch?
    A. Staircase
    B. Too few desks
    C. Sight lines to the chalkboard
    D. Low light
2. What object does Julian show to The Souls at their weekly tea?
    A. A red ball
    B. A cruise ship
    C. An ivory monkey
    D. A book
3. What project–other than stripping wallpaper–do The Souls undertake?
    A. To help Mrs. Olinski
    B. Learn soccer
    C. Learn to play the piano
    D. Build the set for *Annie*

Julian Narrates When Ginger Played Annie's Sandy
1. What do Noah and Nadia bicker about at the Thanksgiving Saturday tea?
    A. Who should be captain of the academic bowl team
    B. Who is the best soccer player
    C. Ginger's ability to play Sandy
    D. Noah's willingness to become an actor
2. What is Nadia's dog's name?
    A. Arnold
    B. Sandy
    C. Ginger
    D. Froelich
3. What important trick does Julian teach The Souls in order to train Ginger?
    A. Heel
    B. Palming treats
    C. Dog whispering
    D. Massage
4. Whose dog does Ginger compete against for the part of Sandy?
    A. Michael Froelich's
    B. Ham Knapp's
    C. Noah Gershom's
    D. Ethan Potter's

The View From Saturday Multiple Choice Study/Quiz Questions Page 11

5. Whose presence at rehearsal is Julian concerned about?
    A. The acting coach's
    B. Nadia's
    C. Ginger's
    D. Michael's
6. Who were the first paying guests at Sillington House?
    A. The Gershoms
    B. Allen Diamondstein and Nadia
    C. The Souls
    D. Izzy and Margaret
7. What does Julian overhear Ham Knapp discussing during the ride to the matinee?
    A. His love for *Annie*
    B. His parents' new home
    C. His plan to tranquilize Ginger
    D. His mother's new cat
8. What is Ham's mother's profession?
    A. Dentist
    B. Teacher
    C. Doctor
    D. Veterinarian
9. How does Julian secretly communicate with The Souls at the matinee?
    A. Sign language
    B. Year-of-the-Souls pennies
    C. Walkie-Talkies
    D. Morse Code
10. What news does Nadia tell Julian about Ginger's performance?
    A. Arnold will be performing instead of Ginger.
    B. Ginger has gotten very sick and can't perform.
    C. Ginger has run out of the building and can't perform.
    D. Nadia is sick and needs Julian to get Ginger ready.
11. What dilemma is Julian faced with?
    A. Whether to help get Ginger ready for the show or not
    B. Whether to stay for the matinee or go home
    C. Whether to prevent Arnold from consuming the dangerous treats
    D. Whether to ask buy a ticket to the opening night performance
12. Why does Mrs. Reynolds become upset with the audience?
    A. They are afraid of the dark.
    B. They act completely inappropriately.
    C. Half of them fall asleep.
    D. They walked out of the auditorium at intermission.

The View From Saturday Multiple Choice Study/Quiz Questions Page 12

13. Why does Mrs. Olinski call Julian aside following the performance?
    A. She thinks he spiked the treats.
    B. She knows he was getting Ginger ready.
    C. She wants to know where Nadia is.
    D. She wants to give Julian a ride to Sillington House.
14. How does Julian resolve his dilemma over the doggie treats?
    A. He decides to spike the treats.
    B. He announces the truth to the audience during intermission.
    C. He removes the dangerous treats from the vicinity of the dogs.
    D. He decides to change brands.

The View From Saturday Multiple Choice Study/Quiz Questions Page 13

Chapter 5
1. How did Mrs. Olinski select her academic bowl team?
    A. Alphabetically
    B. She appointed them.
    C. She drew from a hat.
    D. She asked for volunteers.
2. Which two individuals did Mrs. Olinski choose between to become the fourth member of her team?
    A. Ham Knapp and Julian Singh
    B. Ethan Potter and Nadia Diamondstein
    C. Ham Knapp and Michael Froelich
    D. Noah Gershom and Ham Knapp
3. Why was she reluctant to choose Julian?
    A. She thought he was lazy.
    B. She thought he was moving away.
    C. She didn't think he would work well on a team.
    D. She wanted to choose a girl.
4. Who pushes Mrs. Olinski's wheelchair to the entrance to Sillington House?
    A. She does
    B. Margaret Draper
    C. Izzy Diamondstein
    D. Mr. Singh
5. What unusual thing does Mrs. Olinski observe about the four sixth graders at Sillington House?
    A. They are courteaous and polite with one another.
    B. They always dress alike.
    C. They all have the same middle name.
    D. They sing beautifully together.
6. What two realizations does Mrs. Olinski make at the close of this chapter?
    A. She doesn't like tea or cucumber sandwiches.
    B. She is tired of teaching and wants to move.
    C. She is allergic to trees and milk.
    D. She knows who her fourth member of the team will be, and she knows she will come back to tea.

The View From Saturday Multiple Choice Study/Quiz Questions Page 14

Chapter 6
1. Who wins the competition between Epiphany's sixth grade and seventh grade teams?
    A. Sixth grade
    B. Seventh grade
    C. Eighth grade
2. Which grade do the seventh graders decide to support?
    A. Sixth grade
    B. Seventh grade
    C. Eighth grade
3. Who wins the competition against the eighth graders?
    A. Sixth grade
    B. Seventh grade
    C. Eighth grade

The View From Saturday Multiple Choice Study/Quiz Questions Page 15

Chapter 7

1. How does the team respond to Julian's defiance of the commissioner?
    - A. They are horrified.
    - B. They apologize.
    - C. They support him.
    - D. They pretend not to know him.
2. What action does the commissioner take?
    - A. He leaves the building.
    - B. None–he is speechless.
    - C. He cries.
    - D. He resigns.
3. Who is Mr. LeDue?
    - A. Principal of Knightsbridge
    - B. Principal of Maxwell
    - C. Principal of Epiphany
    - D. Principal of Sillington
4. What is Dr. Rohmer's state of mind?
    - A. He is worried.
    - B. He is happy.
    - C. He is scared.
    - D. He is angry.
5. Which of the following is Dr. Rohmer NOT concerned about before the competition?
    - A. His contract renewal
    - B. Mrs. Olinksi's health
    - C. The district playoffs
    - D. Fairbain's performance
6. Who is Mr. Homer Fairbain?
    - A. Deputy superintendent in charge of instruction
    - B. Commisioner of education
    - C. Julian's uncle
    - D. The tea shop owner
7. Why does Dr. Rohmer feel this year's competition will draw a larger audience?
    - A. It's televised.
    - B. A new library will be built at the winning school.
    - C. It's the final year the competition will be held.
    - D. Everyone wants to see Homer Fairbain make mistakes.
8. How do the sixth graders react when Epiphany beats Knightsbridge?
    - A. They pin pieces of rope on their shirts like medals.
    - B. They hug each other.
    - C. They plan a special tea at Sillington House to celebrate.
    - D. They dedicate their win to Mrs. Olinski.

The View From Saturday Multiple Choice Study/Quiz Questions Page 16

Chapter 8
1. How many regions are there in the state?
    A. 9
    B. 8
    C. 7
    D. 6
2. Why do The Souls decline a Saturday practice at the school?
    A. They are tired of practicing.
    B. They are going to be out of town.
    C. They have tea every Saturday.
    D. They are quitting the team.
3. What is Mrs. Olinski's response?
    A. She becomes angry and send them from the school.
    B. She decides to quit coaching the team.
    C. She shrugs her shoulders.
    D. She joins them for tea.
4. Who greets Mrs. Olinski at her van when she arrives at Sillington House?
    A. Ginger
    B. Mr. Singh
    C. Arnold
    D. The Souls
5. How does Mr. Singh make Mrs. Olinski uneasy?
    A. He asks her on a date.
    B. He knows things about her selection of the team that she has not told anyone.
    C. He asks for her resignation.
    D. He asks about her disability.
6. What is unusual about the question cards that Mr. Singh places in front of Mrs. Olinski?
    A. They are purple.
    B. They are in French.
    C. They are written in calligraphy.
    D. They all pertain to their personal lives.

The View From Saturday Multiple Choice Study/Quiz Questions Page 17

Chapter 9
1. Why does the commissioner of education penalize Julian?
    A. For telling Nadia the answer
    B. For challenging the panel's decision
    C. For leaving in the middle of the competition
    D. For calling the other team names
2. What does the panel discover and tell the commissioner?
    A. Julian's answer is correct.
    B. Julian is not enrolled at Epiphany Middle School.
    C. Julian's answer is incorrect.
    D. Julian is making faces behind the commissioner's back.
3. Why does Dr. Rohmer call a press conference?
    A. For positive publicity
    B. To announce his resignation
    C. To honor the students who participate in the Quiz Bowl
    D. To announce his promotion
4. How is transportation provided for the Epiphany townsfolk to go to Albany?
    A. Tax payer dollars
    B. Dr. Gershom pays for the buses
    C. Money raised from the Century Village T-shirt contributions
    D. It isn't.

The View From Saturday Multiple Choice Study/Quiz Questions Page 18

Chapter 10
1. Who rides with Mrs. Olinski to the competition in Albany?
    A. Ginger
    B. Nadia
    C. The Singhs
    D. Margaret Diamondstein
2. What does the final question of the competition pertain to?
    A. Literature
    B. Weights and Measures
    C. Sports
    D. Music
3. Which team member answers the final question correctly?
    A. Noah
    B. Nadia
    C. Ethan
    D. Julian
4. Which team wins the competition?
    A. Maxwell
    B. Knightsbridge
    C. Epiphany
    D. Albany
5. What is the trophy called?
    A. The big bowl
    B. A loving cup
    C. Shining star
    D. Charlie

The View From Saturday Multiple Choice Study/Quiz Questions Page 19

Chapter 11
1. Who does Mrs. Olinski ask for an explanation regarding her choices for the quiz bowl team?
    A. The Souls
    B. Mrs. Gershom
    C. Julian
    D. Mr. Singh
2. What is his explanation?
    A. They have all been on a journey.
    B. They were the smartest in her class.
    C. It was random chance.
    D. He has no explanation.
3. What have all of The Souls found?
    A. Kindness
    B. A talent
    C. Tea
    D. A pet
4. Which two books did Mrs. Olinski look at just before going to bed after Bowl Day?
    A. *The Bible* and her personal journal
    B. *Alice in Wonderland* and *Through the Looking Glass*
    C. *A Tale of Two Cities* and *Oliver Twist*
    D. *A Midsummer Night's Dream* and *Much Ado About Nothing*

Chapter 12
1. Who opens the door to Sillington House when Mrs. Olinski arrives?
    A. Margaret Draper
    B. Mr. Singh
    C. The Souls
    D. The commissioner
2. What question does Mrs. Olinski ask The Souls when they are seated at their final meeting at Sillington House?
    A. "Can I have a sandwich?"
    B. "Cream or sugar?"
    C. "Did I choose you, or did you choose me?"
    D. "How are you?"
3. What is their response?
    A. "White or wheat?"
    B. "Cream"
    C. "Fine"
    D. "Yes"

ANSWER KEY - MULTIPLE CHOICE STUDY/QUIZ QUESTIONS
The View from Saturday

	Chapter 1	Noah	Chapter 2	Nadia	Chapter 3
1	A	A	D	B	C
2	D	B	D	C	A
3	B	C	A	B	B
4	C	A	C	B	D
5	C	C		A	B
6	B	D		C	C
7	A	D		D	C
8	C	C		B	C
9		C		D	B
10		B		C	A
11		B		D	B
12		A		B	B
13				D	C
14				C	C
15				A	C
16				B	D
17				D	A
18					A
19					C
20					B
21					D

The View from Saturday Multiple Choice Study/Quiz Questions Answer Key Page 2

	Chapter 4	**Julian**	**Chapter 5**	**Chapter 6**	**Chapter 7**
1	C	C	B	A	C
2	C	C	A	A	B
3	A	B	C	A	A
4		A	D		A
5		D	A		B
6		D	D		A
7		C			D
8		D			A
9		B			
10		A			
11		C			
12		B			
13		D			
14		C			

	Chapter 8	**Chapter 9**	**Chapter 10**	**Chapter 11**	**Chapter 12**
1	B	B	C	D	C
2	C	A	A	A	C
3	D	A	D	A	D
4	B	C	C	B	
5	B		B		
6	C				

PREREADING VOCABULARY WORKSHEETS

Vocabulary Worksheet Chapter 1 *The View from Saturday*

Part I: Using Prior Knowledge and Contextual Clues

Below are the sentences in which the vocabulary words appear in the text. Read the sentence. Use any clues you can find in the sentence combined with your prior knowledge, and write what you think the underlined words mean on the lines provided.

1. Whenever she was asked how she had selected her team for the Academic Bowl, she chose one of several good answers . . . Sometimes she said that she knew her team would practice. That was <u>accurate</u>.

   _____

2. Whichever way it began–chicken-or-egg, team-or-The Souls–it <u>definitely</u> ended with an egg.

   _____

3. They were reminded that this Bowl was for brains, not <u>brawn</u>, and decorum–something between chapel and classroom–was the order of the day.

   _____

4. They were reminded that this Bowl was for brains, not brawn, and <u>decorum</u>–something between chapel and classroom–was the order of the day.

   _____

5. At a <u>lectern</u> between them stood the commissioner of education of the state of New York.

   _____

6. He smiled <u>benevolently</u> over the audience as he reached inside his inner breast pocket and withdrew a pair of reading glasses.

   _____

7. Mrs. Olinski hugged her upper arms and wondered if maybe it was nerves and not the <u>quartering</u> wind blowing from the ceiling vents that was causing her shivers.

   _____

8. She watched with <u>bated</u> (and visible) breath as the commissioner placed his hand into a large clear glass bowl.

   _____

The View from Saturday Vocabulary Worksheet Chapter 1 *Continued*

9. Fact: Many of the <u>domiciles</u> in Century Village do not have family rooms with desks.

___

10. Allen Diamondstein kept saying, "Isn't it <u>ironic</u>? My father is getting married just as I am getting divorced."

___

11. The little top layer was totally smashed; it fell in the same puddle as Allen, and the little bride and groom were seriously <u>maimed</u>.

___

Part II: Determining the Meaning
Match the vocabulary words to their dictionary definitions.

```
____  1. accurate          A. homes
____  2. definitely        B. physical strength
____  3. brawn             C. injured permanently
____  4. decorum           D. podium
____  5. lectern           E. etiquette; proper social behavior
____  6. benevolently      F. kindly
____  7. quartering        G. able to cut into fourths
____  8. bated             H. without doubt
____  9. domiciles         I. occurring in a manner opposite to what is expected
____ 10. ironic            J. correct
____ 11. maimed            K. tapered off
```

Vocabulary Worksheet Chapter 2 (Part I) *The View from Saturday*

Part I: Using Prior Knowledge and Contextual Clues

Below are the sentences in which the vocabulary words appear in the text. Read the sentence. Use any clues you can find in the sentence combined with your prior knowledge, and write what you think the underlined words mean on the lines provided.

1. Both Dr. Rohmer and Mrs. Olinski paid strict attention to the commissioner, the man at the podium.

   _____

2. He wore a navy blue, precision fit pin-striped suit and a white-on-dazzling-white shirt.

   _____

3. Mrs. Olinski was not sure how much the correct amount was, but she knew that if she put a spirit-level to his, they would be exactly right.

   _____

4. He was dressed, brushed, coiffed, and blow-dried not just to be seen but to be looked at.

   _____

5. Dr. Rohmer had announced that he had just completed a three-day workshop on multiculturalism for ed-you-kay-toars.

   _____

6. "In the interest of diversity," she said, "I chose a brunette, a redhead, a blond, and a kid with hair as black as print on paper."

   _____

7. He gave Mrs. Olinski a capsule lecture on what multiculturalism really means.

   _____

8. Mrs. Olinski knew that Nadia Diamondstein was not only incandescently beautiful but was also a star.

   _____

The View from Saturday Vocabulary Worksheet Chapter 2 (Part I) *Continued*

9. "What is the name given to that portion of the North Atlantic Ocean that is noted for its abundance of seaweed, and what is its importance to the ecology of our planet?"

_____

Part II: Determining the Meaning
Match the vocabulary words to their dictionary definitions

____ 1. strict
____ 2. precision
____ 3. spirit-level
____ 4. coiffed
____ 5. multiculturalism
____ 6. diversity
____ 7. capsule
____ 8. incandescently
____ 9. ecology

A. compact and succinct
B. glowingly
C. a branch of biology that examines the relationship of organisms to one another and their environment
D. variety
E. characterized by carefully styled, immaculate hairdo
F. exact in detail
G. without relaxation or distraction
H. pertaining to a variety of cultural groups
I. a device that measures evenness

Vocabulary Worksheet Chapter 2 (Part II) *The View from Saturday*

Part I: Using Prior Knowledge and Contextual Clues

Below are the sentences in which the vocabulary words appear in the text. Read the sentence. Use any clues you can find in the sentence combined with your prior knowledge, and write what you think the underlined words mean on the lines provided.

1. Whatever it says on the calendar, Florida has de facto summer.

_____

2. Dad always was a nervous person, but since the divorce he had become terminally so.

_____

3. For the first day and a half after I arrived, Dad hovered over me like the Goodyear blimp over the Orange Bowl.

_____

4. Like all the others, Margaret dresses atrociously. She wears pastel-colored pantsuits with elastic waists or white slacks with overblouses of bright, bold prints.

_____

5. On Sunday we went out for brunch at one of those mammoth places where the menu is small and the portions are large, and every senior citizen leaves with a Styrofoam box containing leftovers.

_____

6. I concluded that many friendships are born and maintained for purely geographical reasons.

_____

7. He looked over at Ethan, inviting him to reinforce the invitation. Ethan nodded slightly.

_____

8. [Ginger] had to fly as baggage. We were advised to tranquilize her and put her in a dog carrier.

_____

The View from Saturday Vocabulary Worksheet Chapter 2 (Part II) *Continued*

9. [Ginger] had to fly as baggage. We were advised to tranquilize her and put her in a dog carrier.

_____

10. Watching a nest hatch is more interesting than digging one out after they've hatched, which is really only a matter of keeping inventory and making certain that everything that was or is living is cleared out.

_____

11. Dad was so preoccupied with time that he did not even notice the sarcasm in my voice.

_____

12. So, there they are, once again at the water's edge, but this time they are without a mechanism for swimming east.

_____

Part II: Determining the Meaning
Match the vocabulary words to their dictionary definitions

___ 1. de facto   A. extremely badly
___ 2. terminally   B. lingered without purpose
___ 3. hovered   C. existing in fact
___ 4. atrociously   D. irreversibly
___ 5. mammoth   E. consumed by the thought of something
___ 6. concluded   F. strengthen
___ 7. reinforce   G. huge
___ 8. advised   H. administer a drug that will soothe or calm
___ 9. tranquilize   I. a list of the quantity of particular items contained in an area
___ 10. inventory   J. an method or instinct an animal has for finding its way
___ 11. preoccupied   K. decided through reasoning and deliberation
___ 12. mechanism   L. offered advice; recommended

Vocabulary Worksheet Chapter 3 (Part 1) *The View from Saturday*

Part I: Using Prior Knowledge and Contextual Clues

Below are the sentences in which the vocabulary words appear in the text. Read the sentence. Use any clues you can find in the sentence combined with your prior knowledge, and write what you think the underlined words mean on the lines provided.

1. When Eva Marie saw that Ethan Potter was assigned to her homeroom, she <u>refrained</u> from asking Margy about him or Ethan about her.

   _____

2. It was an unwritten rule that the seat you chose the first day became your assignment–unless you were so <u>unruly</u> that Mrs. Korshak made you change.

   _____

3. I placed my backpack on the seat next to me, and as <u>nonchalantly</u> as I could, placed my leg over that.

   _____

4. In the family <u>archive</u>, which my Grandmother Draper passed on to my mother when she moved to Florida, there is a letter from her, post-marked Seneca Falls and dated 1848.

   _____

5. None of the historical residents of Epiphany liked the idea of having the Sillington place <u>parceled</u> off for a subdivision.

   _____

6. The main feature of the first floor is the dining room, which stretches from the front of the house to the back because in the days when the Sillington place was a working farm, Mrs. Sillington used to feed all the <u>itinerant</u> farmhands breakfast and supper.

   _____

7. The house itself is perched atop a <u>knoll</u>, and from the upstairs windows you get a good view of the lake.

   _____

8. For a single moment of <u>neglect</u>, I would be stuck with having this kid as a bus partner for the rest of the school year.

   _____

The View from Saturday Vocabulary Worksheet Chapter 3 (Part I) *Continued*

9. We must make Sillington House handicap accessible before we are ready for occupancy. Mrs. Gershom was most helpful in getting permits for the <u>conversion</u>.

_____

10. When the bus stopped, in a <u>feeble</u> attempt to postpone the inevitable, I pretended to be looking for something.

_____

11. When the bus stopped, in a feeble attempt to postpone the <u>inevitable</u>, I pretended to be looking for something.

_____

Part II: Determining the Meaning
Match the vocabulary words to their dictionary definitions

____ 1. refrained
____ 2. unruly
____ 3. nonchalantly
____ 4. archive
____ 5. parceled
____ 6. itinerant
____ 7. knoll
____ 8. neglect
____ 9. conversion
____ 10. feeble
____ 11. inevitable

A. hard to control
B. a small hill
C. inattention
D. kept oneself from doing something
E. traveling
F. weak
G. a collection of historical documents or records
H. in a relaxed and laid-back manner; unconcerned
I. divided into smaller units
J. certain, with an unavoidable outcome
K. something that has changed into another form, substance, state, or product

Vocabulary Worksheet Chapter 3 (Part II) *The View from Saturday*

Part I: Using Prior Knowledge and Contextual Clues

Below are the sentences in which the vocabulary words appear in the text. Read the sentence. Use any clues you can find in the sentence combined with your prior knowledge, and write what you think the underlined words mean on the lines provided.

1. They stuck their feet into the aisle of the bus to trip him as he made his way toward the back, but even though he seemed to have his eyes focused straight ahead, he managed to stop just short of the <u>protruding</u> feet...

   _____

2. Their next form of <u>torment</u> was to repeat whatever Julian said in an exaggerated imitation of his accent.

   _____

3. He <u>disentangled</u> his arm and started toward Ham, but now his way was blocked by Michael, running backward, waving his arms like a guard in a game of basketball.

   _____

4. Mr. Singh stepped aside to allow Julian and Noah to <u>precede</u> him up the walk.

   _____

5. Ginger is a genius of her <u>genus</u>. She is the best there is of *Canis familiaris*, and Alice is the best of her litter.

   _____

6. "Mother was an American by birth, Father is by <u>naturalization</u>. I was born on the high seas. That makes me American."

   _____

7. "Let us say that I am as American as pizza pie. I did not <u>originate</u> here, but I am here to stay."

   _____

8. "Calligraphy is a skill I have always wanted to <u>acquire</u>."

   _____

The View from Saturday -Vocabulary Worksheet Chapter 3 (Part II) *Continued*

9. Something there triggered the unfolding of those parts that had been <u>incubating</u>.

_____

10. Things that had lain inside me, curled up like the turtle hatchlings newly emerged from their eggs, taking time in the dark of their nest to <u>unfurl</u> themselves.

_____

Part II: Determining the Meaning
Match the vocabulary words to their dictionary definitions

____ 1. protruding   A. in biology, a category above *species* and below *family*
____ 2. torment   B. sticking out
____ 3. disentangled   C. the process of granting citizenship to a foreigner
____ 4. precede   D. have a beginning
____ 5. genus   E. to learn or possess
____ 6. naturalization   F. to spread out from a folded position
____ 7. originate   G. intense suffering
____ 8. acquire   H. untwisted
____ 9. incubating   I. to go before
____ 10. unfurl   J. keeping eggs warm until hatchlings emerge

Vocabulary Worksheet Chapter 4 *The View from Saturday*

Part I: Using Prior Knowledge and Contextual Clues
Below are the sentences in which the vocabulary words appear in the text. Read the sentence. Use any clues you can find in the sentence combined with your prior knowledge, and write what you think the underlined words mean on the lines provided.

1. She wrote it all down, revised, memorized, and rehearsed until she could deliver her lines with a light touch.

2. There was a spontaneous burst of applause from their side of the aisle that was immediately suppressed by the commissioner.

3. There was a spontaneous burst of applause from their side of the aisle that was immediately suppressed by the commissioner

4. "I must admonish the audience not to applaud. It is distracting to both teams."

5. Can you give me two examples of acronyms that have entered our language as words?"

6. We trained Ginger to accept the treat without excessive salivating.

7. We had them all facing the same way so that their shadows on the wall looked like a computer rendering of an architectural cross section.

8. He purchased a beautiful cut glass carafe and matching drinking glass and put them on the nightstand by the bed.

9. Or did she think that I started that ruckus in the auditorium?

The View from Saturday Vocabulary Worksheet Chapter 4 *Continued*

10. I was still so angry that I was about to violate one of the cardinal rules that Gopal had taught me.

_____

Part II: Determining the Meaning
Match the vocabulary words to their dictionary definitions

____ 1. revised   A. occurring without planning or warning
____ 2. spontaneous   B. more than is needed or wanted
____ 3. suppressed   C. version or translation
____ 4. admonish   D. fundamental
____ 5. acronyms   E. reconsidered; altered; amended; improved
____ 6. excessive   F. prevented from being expressed; Kept down
____ 7. rendering   G. warn
____ 8. carafe   H. commotion
____ 9. ruckus   I. word created from the initial letters of words in a longer phrase
____ 10. cardinal   J. a glass receptacle with an open top used for holding water

Vocabulary Chapters 5-6 *The View from Saturday*

Part I: Using Prior Knowledge and Contextual Clues
Below are the sentences in which the vocabulary words appear in the text. Read the sentence. Use any clues you can find in the sentence combined with your prior knowledge, and write what you think the underlined words mean on the lines provided.

1. In the teachers' lounge, Mrs. Sharkey, who taught sixth grade math, accused Mrs. Olinski of being <u>dictatorial</u>, and Ms. Masolino, who taught music and who did not have a homeroom at all, hinted that she was lazy.

   _____

2. She would <u>appoint</u> her team, the way the president appointed his cabinet.

   _____

3. And he was <u>sophisticated</u> (or else his English accent made him seem so).

   _____

4. Mrs. Olinski had a great tolerance for mischief, but she had no patience for <u>malice</u>.

   _____

5. She had always regarded the color turquoise...as the color equivalent of the word *ain't*: <u>quaint</u> when seldom used but vulgar in great doses.

   _____

6. She had always regarded the color turquoise...as the color equivalent f the word *ain't*: quaint when seldom used but <u>vulgar</u> in great doses.

   _____

7. She was on the <u>verge</u> of screaming with pain and rage when she felt her wheelchair begin to move.

   _____

8. The Souls continued their <u>animated</u> conversation, when suddenly, as if on signal, the four of them looked back at Mrs. Olinski.

   _____

The View from Saturday Vocabulary Worksheet Chapters 5-6 *Continued*

9. Mrs. Sharkey said that, after all, she knew the current seventh grade, for she had taught them just last year, and in her opinion, when they were very, very good, they were <u>mediocre</u>.

_____

10. Before he reached the front of the classroom, someone launched another belch. Its sound rocketed forward, and the laughter that followed traveled the same <u>trajectory</u>.

_____

11. As he <u>ambled</u> down his row toward the front of the room, smiling faces lifted and tilted toward him. . . .

_____

12. . . . the four-part question that they answered to win... Mrs. Laurecin was impressed. The sixth grade was <u>jubilant</u>.

_____

Part II: Determining the Meaning
Match the vocabulary words to their dictionary definitions

____	1. dictatorial	A. having worldly experience or culture
____	2. appoint	B. a point or limit
____	3. sophisticated	C. strolled or walked leisurely
____	4. malice	D. charmingly old-fashioned
____	5. quaint	E. the path a flying object takes
____	6. vulgar	F. triumphantly happy
____	7. verge	G. assign people to a certain task or job
____	8. animated	H. lacking charm, culture, or sophistication
____	9. mediocre	I. behaving as if one has complete rule over others
____	10. trajectory	J. wanting to do harm to someone
____	11. ambled	K. average to below average in quality
____	12. jubilant	L. lively

Vocabulary Chapters 7 *The View from Saturday*

Part I: Using Prior Knowledge and Contextual Clues
Below are the sentences in which the vocabulary words appear in the text. Read the sentence. Use any clues you can find in the sentence combined with your prior knowledge, and write what you think the underlined words mean on the lines provided.

1. Any other team on spaceship Earth would have worried about Julian's defying an official of the sovereign state of New York.

2. Then the day before the contest for the district championship Mr. Connor LeDue, the principal of Knightsbridge Middle School, found some pretext to visit Mrs. Olinski.

3. The day after the broadcast, there were five letters to the editor in the paper about Mr. Fairbain, none favorable.

4. Mr. Fairbain did well and actually seemed to be enjoying himself until syllabication did him in.

5. Dr. Rohmer paled to the point of translucence, and the audience gasped.

6. Crushing applause followed a nanosecond of crushing silence.

7. Everyone clapped. But not the sixth-grade sentinels who lined the walls.

8. When The Souls came down off the stage, they stood four abreast behind Mrs. Olinski's wheelchair and pushed her toward the back of the room where the sixth graders converged and formed a phalanx that lifted her...

63

The View from Saturday Vocabulary Worksheet Chapters 7 *Continued*

9. When The Souls came down off the stage, they stood four abreast behind Mrs. Olinski's wheelchair and pushed her toward the back of the room where the sixth graders converged and formed a <u>phalanx</u> that lifted her...

_____

Part II: Determining the Meaning
Match the vocabulary words to their dictionary definitions

____ 1. sovereign   A. having to do with syllables
____ 2. pretext   B. guards who stand to watch over someone or something
____ 3. favorable   C. a king who is supreme ruler
____ 4. syllabication   D. a unit of troops who stand closely together
____ 5. translucence   E. showing approval
____ 6. nanosecond   F. the tiniest fraction of a second
____ 7. sentinels   G. false excuse
____ 8. converged   H. a state of being semi-transparent
____ 9. phalanx   I. came from different directions toward a central point

Vocabulary Chapters 8-12 *The View from Saturday*

Part I: Using Prior Knowledge and Contextual Clues
Below are the sentences in which the vocabulary words appear in the text. Read the sentence. Use any clues you can find in the sentence combined with your prior knowledge, and write what you think the underlined words mean on the lines provided.

1. Mrs. Olinski finished the last of the miniature cream puffs, delicately touched her napkin to the corners of her mouth, folded it, laid it on the table alongside her saucer, lifted her eyes, and saw four smiles <u>adorn</u> the faces opposite her.

   _____

2. Mrs. Olinski gave one of her good answers: her "<u>complementary</u> skills" response, dressing it up to say that the team's talents blended like a chorus, making one sound out of may voices.

   _____

3. He said that unlike football matches where he could charge admission to the games, there was no <u>precedent</u> for charging admission to the Academic Bowl.

   _____

4. Mrs. Olinski smiled and said thank you...over and over again, wheeling her chair in small circles until her smile and her words floated like a <u>frieze</u> around the room.

   _____

5. Finally, almost <u>involuntarily</u>, she said out loud, "Win some. Lose some." She glanced at Mr. Singh and laughed. "Why did I say that?"

   _____

6. "For many months now, you have been in a state of <u>perpetual</u> preparation and excitement. Each victory was a preparation for the next".

   _____

Part II: Determining the Meaning
Match the vocabulary words to their dictionary definitions

____ 1. adorn   A. a previous event that serves as an example in the future
____ 2. complementary   B. continuing without change or end
____ 3. precedent   C. doing something against one's will
____ 4. frieze   D. decorate splendidly
____ 5. involuntarily   E. combining in such a way as to enhance each other
____ 6. perpetual   F. a horizontal band of decoration in a building

VOCABULARY WORKSHEET ANSWER KEY *The View from Saturday*

	Chapter 1	Chapter 2 Part 1	Chapter 2 Part 2	Chapter 3 Part 1	Chapter 3 Part 2
1	J	G	C	D	B
2	H	F	D	A	G
3	B	I	B	H	H
4	E	E	A	G	I
5	D	H	G	I	A
6	F	D	K	E	C
7	G	A	F	B	D
8	K	B	L	C	E
9	A	C	H	K	J
10	I		I	F	F
11	C		E	J	
12			J		

	Chapter 4	Chapters 5-6	Chapter 7	Chapters 8-12
1	E	I	C	D
2	A	G	G	E
3	F	A	E	A
4	G	J	A	F
5	I	D	H	C
6	B	H	F	B
7	C	B	B	
8	J	L	I	
9	H	K	D	
10	D	E		
11		C		
12		F		

DAILY LESSONS

LESSON ONE

Objectives
1. To introduce students to subject matter discussed in the novel
2. To introduce students to a variety of media center resources or online research
2. To distribute the books and other materials necessary for the unit
3. To preview the novel by drawing conclusions from the cover and table of contents

Activity #1

Students should meet in the library for this activity. Alternately, you may choose to conduct this activity on the Internet, which would allow students to hone their computer research skills.

Divide students into 5 groups. Each group should receive a **folded** "Scavenger Hunt" form with three questions on it. *(Note: These questions have been taken directly from the "fifteen questions with thirty-six answers" found at the end of the novel. A question list follows this lesson for your convenience-simply cut the pages and distribute to the appropriate groups. A complete answer key can be found at the back of the novel.)*

When told to begin, the students will have about 15 minutes to answer their three questions. They may go about this any way they see fit. Let them decide how to divide the responsibilities for the task. After time is called, ask the students to come back together as a class to discuss their experience. Then check their answers. Some sample discussion questions follow:

How did each group tackle the challenge?
Did the students work together as a group on each question, or did they divide individual responsibility among the three questions?
How did the groups handle any disagreements that arose?
Do they feel confident that their answers are correct?
Did the group completely finish their assignments in the time allotted?
Were the topics familiar to them?
Were they able to answer any of the questions without consulting outside sources?
What were the most difficult questions?
What were the most interesting questions?
Did their research leave them with further questions?

TRANSITION: "In E.L. Konigsburg's novel *The View from Saturday,* we are going to read about a group of students who build friendships and participate in an Academic Quiz Bowl, which tests students' ability to answer questions on a variety of topics like the ones you researched today. Throughout this unit, you will also have an opportunity to form a group and explore a hobby, craft, subject, or issue that is of common interest to you and your group members.

The View From Saturday Lesson One Continued

Activity #2
Distribute the materials students will use in this unit. Explain in detail how students are to use these materials.

Study Guides Students should read the study guide questions for each reading assignment prior to beginning the reading assignment to get a feeling for what events and ideas are important in the section they are about to read. After reading the section, students will (as a class or individually) answer the questions to review the important events and ideas from that section of the book. Students should keep the study guides as study materials for the unit test.

Vocabulary Prior to each reading assignment, students will do vocabulary work related to the section of the book they are about to read. Following the completion of the reading of the book, there will be a vocabulary review of all the words used in the vocabulary assignments. Students should keep their vocabulary work as study materials for the unit test.

Reading Assignment Sheet You need to fill in the reading assignment sheet to let students know by when their reading has to be completed. You can either write the assignment sheet up on a side blackboard or bulletin board and leave it there for students to see each day, or you can "ditto" copies for each student to have. In either case, you should advise students to become very familiar with the reading assignments so they know what is expected of them.

Extra Activities Center The Unit Resource Materials portion of this LitPlan contains suggestions for an extra library of related books and articles in your classroom as well as crossword and word search puzzles. Make an extra activities center in your room where you will keep these materials for students to use. (Bring the books and articles in from the library and keep several copies of the puzzles on hand.) Explain to students that these materials are available for students to use when they finish reading assignments or other class work early.

Nonfiction Assignment Sheet Explain to students that they each are to read at least one non-fiction piece from the in-class library at some time during the unit. Students will fill out a nonfiction assignment sheet after completing the reading to help you (the teacher) evaluate their reading experiences and to help the students think about and evaluate their own reading experiences.

Books Each school has its own rules and regulations regarding student use of school books. Advise students of the procedures that are normal for your school. Preview the book. Look at the covers, front-matter, and index. Glance through at some of the drawings.

The View From Saturday Lesson One Continued

<u>Activity #3</u>
      Give students the opportunity to look at the book cover, table of contents, and illustrations with their group members from Activity #1. As a class, discuss: "what do you think this book will be about? What are your predictions about *The View from Saturday*? You may decide to post responses on individual paper strips on the bulletin board, or you may use the topic as a prompt for a journal entry. You may also decide to list any questions that the students generate about the novel.

SCAVENGER HUNT QUESTIONS *The View From Saturday*

Group 1
What is the meaning of the word *calligraphy* and from what language does it derive?

What is the name given to that portion of the North Atlantic Ocean that is noted for its abundance of seaweed, and what is its importance to the ecology of our planet?

What famous American women are associated with the following places in New York State and why are they important?
    Seneca Falls
    Homer
    Rochester
    Auburn

Group 2
How many quarters are in twenty dollars?

If one man can paint an eight feet by twelve feet wall in a half hour, how long would it take three men to paint a wall that is eight feet by twenty-four feet?

A masterpiece by the artist Rembrandt was recently stolen from a museum in his native country. What is that country? What is its capital?

Group 3
Name the parts of the human eye in the order that light reaches them.

Name the famous fathers of:
    Queen Elizabeth I of England
    Esau and Jacob
    Alexander the Great
    Our country

What is the origin of the phrase, "to meet one's Waterloo" and what does it mean?

The View From Saturday Scavenger Hunt Questions Continued

Group 4
Name the tribe associated with each of the following Native American leaders and name a major accomplishment of one.
    Sequoyah
    Tecumseh
    Osceola
    Geronimo

What is SONAR an acronym for?

Who was the first president to live in the White House?

Group 5
What is the waste product of photosynthesis?

Name the three major food groups.

Who was the first Spanish explorer to reach Florida?

NONFICTION ASSIGNMENT SHEET
The View From Saturday
(To be completed after reading the required nonfiction article)

Name _____ Date _____

Title of Nonfiction Read _____

Written By _____ Publication Date _____

I. Factual Summary: Write a short summary of the piece you read.

II. Vocabulary
    1. With which vocabulary words in the piece did you encounter some degree of difficulty?

    2. How did you resolve your lack of understanding with these words?

III. Interpretation: What was the main point the author wanted you to get from reading his work?

IV. Criticism
    1. With which points of the piece did you agree or find easy to accept? Why?

    2. With which points of the piece did you disagree or find difficult to believe? Why?

V. Personal Response: What do you think about this piece? <u>OR</u> How does this piece influence your ideas?

LESSON TWO

Objectives
1. To familiarize students with the study guide questions for Chapter 1
2. To familiarize students with vocabulary for Chapter 1
3. To read Chapter 1
4. To give students practice reading orally
5. To evaluate students' oral reading

Activity #1
Tell students to look at their study questions for Chapter 1 of *The View From Saturday*. Read through them orally as a class, choosing different students to read each question. Explain to students that they should read through the study questions prior to reading each assignment to get a feeling for what ideas are important as they come across them in their reading. Advise students that they will have to write the answers to these questions after their reading is completed.

Activity #2
Tell students to look at the vocabulary worksheet for Chapter 1. Explain that in Part I they are to read the sentence and through any contextual clues and prior knowledge, guess what the word means and write their response on the line provided. Do each one as a class. Explain that in Part II they are to match the words with their dictionary definitions. Do this orally as a class and have students write in the correct answers. Explain that in the future, they will do these worksheets independently.

Activity #3
Have students read Chapter 1 of *The View from Saturday* aloud in class. You probably know the best way to select readers in your classroom; pick students at random, ask for volunteers, or use whatever method works best for your group. If you have not yet completed an oral reading evaluation for your students this period, this would be a good opportunity to do so. A form is included with this unit for your convenience. If students do not finish reading Chapter 1 in class, they complete this assignment for homework.

ORAL READING EVALUATION *The View From Saturday*

Name _____ Class____ Date _____

SKILL	EXCELLENT	GOOD	AVERAGE	FAIR	POOR
Fluency	5	4	3	2	1
Clarity	5	4	3	2	1
Audibility	5	4	3	2	1
Pronunciation	5	4	3	2	1
_____	5	4	3	2	1
_____	5	4	3	2	1

Total _____ Grade _____

Comments:

LESSON THREE

<u>Objectives</u>
1. To review the main events and ideas from Chapter 1
2. To introduce students to the group project & form groups
3. To give students time to begin organizing their project work

<u>Activity #1</u>
Give students a few minutes to formulate answers for the study guide questions for Chapter 1, and then discuss the answers to the questions in detail. Write the answers on the board or overhead transparency so students can have the correct answers for study purposes.

Note: It is a good practice in public speaking and leadership skills for individual students to take charge of leading the discussions of the study questions. Perhaps a different student could go to the front of the class and lead the discussion each day that the study questions are discussed during this unit. Of course, the teacher should guide the discussion when appropriate and be sure to fill in any gaps the students leave.

<u>Activity #2</u>
Tell students to take a few minutes to brainstorm things they have always wanted to learn about. It could be a skill, sport, hobby, or craft; a person, subject, place or issue that has intrigued them; a musical group, an author or kind of literature–any topic of interest.

Give students a minute of silence to think about their personal interests.

Then, ask students to share things they brain-stormed. Write some of the topics on the board or overhead.

<u>Activity #3</u>
Based on the list you have accumulated from student responses, try to match students with common interests. (Look for any "Oh, yeah, me, too!" moments!) Create (ideally) groups of 4 or 5 members with a common interest and have them rearrange themselves in the classroom so the group members are together.

Explain to the class that in the book *The View From Saturday,* the sixth grade academic bowl team turned into a group of friends who met on their own outside of school. For this project, groups with similar interests have been assembled. Each group will research its topic, write a paper about the topic, create a project relating to the topic, and compose relevant questions (with answers) that would be appropriate for an academic bowl game. The interaction of the group members in accomplishing the tasks is as important as the tasks being done, to give students an appreciation for how closely The Souls worked together.

<u>Activity #4</u>
Distribute the Project Outline Guides, one for each group member plus an extra one for students to fill out for you. Tell students to use this class time to discuss the questions and complete the outline guide. Tell students that their outline guides will be due at the end of the next class period.

PROJECT OUT LINE GUIDE
The View From Saturday

PROMPT
The View From Saturday is a book about, among other things, four sixth graders who form special friendships through their participation as an academic bowl game team. They did most of their preparation for the competitions after school hours, and in doing so, they learned more than just the facts for the competitions. They learned about each other, they learned how to do new things, and they were exposed to new ideas. Each member had an individual journey as the group melded into The Souls.

THE ASSIGNMENT
You have been placed in groups with members who have something in common. Your assignment is to work together in your group to explore the topic of your common interest. Much of the work for this assignment will have to be done outside of class, but you will have some class time to get started.

Your assignment is to explore your topic of common interest, write a paper about it, create a project (something that can be experienced through one or more senses), and write 15 questions about your topic that could be used in an academic bowl game.

PROMPT
It is up to you to decide how you will explore your topic, how you will get the paper written, what project you will complete and how you will complete it, and how you will choose and write your 15 bowl game questions. Part of the point of the assignment is for you to share ideas with each other and make decisions together, as The Souls did.

SCHEDULE
Your written composition about your topic is due on _____.
You will share your completed project with the class on _____.
Your 15 academic bowl questions must be ready by _____.

GETTING STARTED
As a means of getting started, complete the worksheet on the following page. Answering these questions will help you to start thinking about the tasks ahead and how you might get them completed. *This is only a starting point.* The rest is up to you to complete by the assigned dates.

PROBLEMS? QUESTIONS?
Try to solve your issues within the group. If you cannot resolve a problem or truly require outside help or intervention, let me know.

GROUP PROJECT OUTLINE GUIDE WORKSHEET
The View From Saturday

List the group members here:

State the group project topic here:

What might your final product be?

What resources would you need to complete your project?

What kinds of information should you include in your paper?

How will you divide the responsibilities of completing the project and paper?

What will each group member's responsibilities be? List each person's name and write a description of that person's duties next to his/her name.

What questions do you have?

LESSON FOUR

Objectives
    1. To preview and read Chapter 2, Part 1
    2. To give students the opportunity to complete organizing their group projects

Activity #1

Give students approximately fifteen minutes to work in their groups, to complete the project outline guide. Collect your copies from the groups.

Activity #2

Tell students to take a few minutes to look at the 4 study guide questions for the first part of Chapter 2 (prior to Nadia Tells of Turtle Love), to complete the vocabulary worksheet for Chapter 2 Part 1, and to silently, independently read that first part of Chapter 2 (up to–not including–Nadia Tells of Turtle Love). If students do not complete this assignment in class, they should finish it for homework.

LESSON FIVE

Objectives
1. To check students' work from Chapter 2, Part 1
2. To preview and read Chapter 2, Part 2 (Nadia Tells of Turtle Love)

Activity #1
Tell students to take out a half sheet of paper, write their usual class heading (name, class, date, etc.) on the top, and number the page from 1-4. Write (or have written) on the board or overhead transparency the four multiple choice study questions for the first part of Chapter 2. Tell students to write the letters of the correct answers for each question on their papers. Give students ample time to complete this assignment, and then have students swap papers for in-class grading. Students should write the correct answer next to any incorrect ones given. Collect the quizzes so you can see how students did. Be sure to return the quizzes after recording grades (if you choose to do so) so students have the correct answers for study purposes.

Activity #2
Students should read over the study guide questions for Nadia Tells of Turtle Love in order to get a feel for the reading assignment. Tell students to also complete the vocabulary worksheet for that section of the book. Give students about fifteen minutes to work on the vocabulary worksheet (Chapter 2 Part II) and then discuss the answers orally in class.

Activity #3
Have students begin reading Nadia Tells of Turtle Love aloud in class. If students do not finish reading this portion of the book in class, they should do so prior to the next class meeting.

LESSON SIX

Objectives
1. To review the main events and ideas from Chapter 2, Part 2 (Nadia Tells of Turtle Love)
2. To preview and read part Chapter 3, Part 1
3. To complete the oral reading evaluations

Activity #1
Distribute or tell students to pull out their study questions for Nadia Tells of Turtle Love, from Chapter 2. Take a few minutes to discuss the answers to these questions with your class.

Activity #2
Have students look at the study questions for the first part of Chapter 3 and complete the vocabulary worksheet for that portion of the book. Students may either do this independently or orally as a class–whichever you think is best. If they do it independently, be sure to discuss the answers to the vocabulary worksheet so all students know the correct answers.

Activity #3
If you have not yet completed the oral reading evaluations for all students in your class, have students read the first part of Chapter 3 orally so you can complete the evaluations. If you have completed the evaluations already (or have opted not to do the evaluations), students may read this portion of the book silently in the remainder of this class period. This reading assignment must be completed prior to the next class meeting.

NOTE: If students read independently and finish reading prior to the end of the class, they should quietly work on their group projects. If several students from the same group finish reading, they may quietly work together to discuss their project.

LESSON SEVEN

Objectives
1. To give students time to work on their group projects
2. To preview Chapter 3, Part 2 (Ethan Explains the B and B Inn)

Activity #1

Take students to the library/media center to find articles, books, etc. about their project group assignment. Each group should use a minimum of three sources in their research. Appropriately documented Internet sources are acceptable.

Suggest that students begin by dividing their responsibilities. For example, one member might be responsible for searching on the computer while another may look through books pertaining to the subject. Other members may brainstorm sub-topics related to their main topic.

Since the process of working in a group and establishing a group dynamic is as important to understanding this particular novel as the final product the group produces, allow students to explore and establish their own guidelines whenever feasible.

Activity#2

Tell students that prior to the next class period they should preview the study questions and do the vocabulary worksheet for the second part of Chapter 3 (Ethan Explains the B and B Inn). If any students finish their portions of the group research before the end of the class period, they should begin working on this assignment.

LESSON EIGHT

Objectives
1. To review the vocabulary worksheet for Chapter 3, Part 2 (Ethan Explains the B & B Inn)
2. To complete reading Chapter 3, Part 2 (Ethan Explains the B and B Inn)

Activity#1

Discuss the answers to the vocabulary worksheet for this section of the novel so all students have the correct answers.

Activity #2

Students should use the remainder of the class period to read Ethan Explains the B and B Inn. This assignment must be completed prior to the next class meeting. If students finish early, they may work on their group project assignments.

LESSON NINE

Objectives
1. To give students time to work on their group projects
2. To evaluate students' ability to write a friendly thank you letter
3. To connect the book to students' lives
4. To explore the themes of kindness and courtesy in the novel

Activity #1
Tell students that the themes of kindness and courtesy are important in the novel. Ask students to think about the parts of the book they have read so far–and look back at their notes/study guides if necessary–and suggest things that have related to these themes.

Some examples might be Noah's B&B letter, Tillie's teaching Noah calligraphy, the gift invitations, helping the turtles, Margaret's setting up Nadia's mother's job interview, Ethan's sharing his bus seat with Julian, the gifts taken to the tea party, etc.

Activity #2
Explain to students that in our busy, technological world we tend to overlook being kind and courteous–and to overlook many thank-yous to people who are kind to us. Some times we may pick up the phone or shoot a quick e-mail to say, "Thanks," but too often we don't really take the time to give people a proper, "Thank you."

Noah's mother makes him write a thank you note–a Bread and Butter letter–to his grandparents. He stops and carefully considers the events of his visit and what he received. Then he starts to write his letter.

Distribute Writing Assignment #1, discuss the directions in detail, and give students ample time to complete the assignment. Tell students when you will collect the papers.

NOTE: It would be a good idea to write a complete thank you note in the correct form on the board or on an overhead transparency so students can see the proper form to use and have a complete note as a guide. A sample follows the writing assignment.

Activity#3
If time remains in the class period or some students finish early, students may continue working on their group projects.

WRITING ASSIGNMENT #1 *The View From Saturday*

PROMPT
"I let my pen drink up a whole plunger full of ink and then holding the pen over the bottle, I squeezed three drops back into the bottle.

And I thought–a B & B letter is giving just a few drops back to the bottle."

The first chapter of the novel closes with this quote from Noah as he begins writing a note of thanks to his grandparents at Century Village.

Think about a time when someone showed you hospitality or kindness. What impact did that kindness have on your life? Give a few drops back to the bottle by writing a thank you letter to that person (or persons) and letting him/her know how much you appreciate his/her kindness.

PREWRITING
You may begin by making a list of items people have given to you or kindnesses people have shown you. Look back over your list. Which of these made the greatest impact on your life? Have these people gone unthanked? After choosing the recipient of your letter, brainstorm the ways that person made your life better. Think about Noah's prewriting activity in the novel.

DRAFTING
Since you are writing a letter, you should use standard letter form. When you thank the recipient of this letter, be sure to be specific when explaining the way they made your life richer, or how they might have inspired you to pass along that kindness to someone else.

PEER CONFERENCING/REVISING
When you finish the rough draft of your paper, ask a student who sits near you to read it. After reading your rough draft, he/she should tell you what he/she liked best about your work, which parts were difficult to understand, and ways in which your work could be improved. Reread your paper considering your critic's comments, and make the corrections you think are necessary.

PROOFREADING
Do a final proofreading of your paper double-checking your grammar, spelling, organization, and the clarity of your ideas.

SAMPLE THANK YOU LETTER *The View From Saturday*

July 17, 2006

Dear Aunt Ethel,

 I wanted to take a minute to tell you how much I enjoyed the email you sent with the picture attached. The story you told about Mom and you getting locked out of the house when you were kids was really funny! I especially liked the attached photo of you and Mom as kids. I think I'll print out your email and the picture to put in my scrapbook so I can enjoy both for many years to come.
 Sometimes I forget to tell you how much I appreciate all the little things like this that you send me and the little things you do for me. You're a great aunt!

           Love,
           Keith

LESSON TEN

Objectives
    1. To review the main events and ideas from Chapter 3
    2. To preview and read Chapters 4, 5, and 6

Activity #1
    Tell students to look at their study questions for Chapter 3. Discuss the answers in detail and make sure all students have the correct answers written down for studying purposes.

Activity #2
Note: Essentially, students will be completing the same work for Chapters 4-6 as they did for the previous chapters; however, they will be reading and studying Chapters 4-6 in their project groups in order to mimic the cohesion of The Souls in the novel and provide a real-life connection to the characters' experiences (while also easing the possible monotony of daily oral reading). You may need to alter or enhance this approach, depending on your own class needs.

Divide students into groups. Explain to them that they will be responsible for previewing the study guide questions for chapters 4-6, completing the vocabulary worksheets for chapters 4-6, reading chapters 4-6, and answering the study guide questions for chapters 4-6. Each group will determine how to accomplish these tasks, what each group member's responsibility will be, which work will be completed in class, and how reading assignments will be completed. All of the work must be finished by the beginning of class on (date for Lesson 11). Circulate through the classroom and talk with individual groups over the next two days to maintain order and clarify any points of confusion the students may have throughout the group study. This is also a good time to discuss the novel with smaller numbers of students and get their reactions to the text.

You may choose to complete this activity in one class period or two, depending on how well your students work in groups and the ability level(s) of your students. Or, you may choose this approach with some of the longer chapters instead. If students have extra time, they should review the study guide questions or vocabulary from the novel.

LESSON ELEVEN

Objectives
1. To review the main events and ideas from Chapters 4-6
2. To preview and read Chapter 7

Activity #1
    Tell students to look at their study questions for Chapters 4-6. Discuss the answers in detail and make sure all students have the correct answers written down for studying purposes.

Activity #2
    Tell students to read through their study questions, do the vocabulary worksheets for, and read Chapter 7. Give them the rest of this class period to work on this assignment, which should be completed prior to the next class meeting.

Homework: Students should bring in a sample of a list of instructions (assembly instructions, a recipe, driving directions, etc.) for use in the next class meeting.

LESSON TWELVE

Objectives
1. To review the main events and ideas from Chapter 7
2. To gauge students' ability to follow directions
3. To examine detailed instructional writing
4. To practice writing a clear, organized, detailed set of instructions.

Activity #1
    Tell students to look at the study questions for Chapter 7. Discuss the answers in detail and make sure students write the correct answers for studying purposes.

Activity #2
Without any explanation, give each student a copy of the half sheet of instructions which follows this lesson(there are actually two copies per page; simply copy and cut on the dotted lines). Be sure that the paper remains **face down** on each student's desk until you tell the class to begin. Tell students they will have about 5 minutes to complete the worksheet. Instruct students to wait patiently and quietly when they are finished to give everyone ample time to complete the assignment.

After all students have finished, discuss the activity. If all students follow the instructions correctly, they should not have done anything to the hand-out. How many students are standing beside their desks? How many have desk tops adorned with paper airplanes? How many wrote their names on their papers before realizing that they should read through all of the steps first? What does this tell us? Under what circumstances might such an error have more dire consequences than they did today? Allow students to share relevant personal experiences.

Post the following quotes from the novel on the board. Discuss these quotes with the class in relation to the completion of tasks and achievement of goals. Do you think Tillie's six steps are more than is necessary? Brainstorm other activities where the preparation is essential to the success of the activity itself (i.e. painting/prepping, running/stretching, cooking/measuring).

"Now, Mr. Knapp and Mr. Lord," she said, "I would like the two of you to teach the entire class how to belch on command. Please describe the process for all of us." . . . Which one of you wants to take notes on the instructions we are about to receive? (129)

"You must think of those six steps not as preparation for the beginning, but as the beginning itself." (p. 10)

The View From Saturday Lesson Twelve Continued

Activity #3
Ask students to pull out the examples of instructions they brought in for homework. Categorize the various types on the board. *(Note: It might be helpful to bring in samples of your own, such as recipes, directions printed off of Mapquest, instructions for assembling furniture, instructions for playing a game, etc.)* After students have listed their samples, have them divide into groups according to type– some examples may be RECIPES, DRIVING DIRECTIONS, GAME INSTRUCTIONS, OTHER.

Direct students to discuss the following aspects of their examples (*you may want to write these on the board or overhead*)
Discuss similarities and differences among the examples in your group. Discuss the specifics and details. Are some samples more detailed than others? Are the more detailed instructions better than those that are more general?
Discuss possible pitfalls or ambiguities in the instructions. What would happen if certain steps were eliminated?
Do you consider each of the examples to be well-written? Would you be able to accomplish the given task with this list and no other information?

Students should answer the following questions to turn in as documentation of their discussion and homework completion:
What is the source of your sample (where did you find it?)
Who do you think is the intended audience (adult or child? Professional or novice?)
For common tasks, are their certain assumptions that WE ALL make? Explain. (i.e., driving directions will not tell us to stop at a stop sign before turning right at that stop sign. We are working under a different set of instructions that tell us that a stop sign always means stop first, turn after.)

Activity #3 (Homework if time does not permit in class)
Each student will write a set of instructions for a specific task. Students may select a topic or you may offer suggestions, such as:
Walk from your desk to the secretary's desk in the main office.
Prepare your favorite meal.
Play your favorite game.

When students have completed the assignment have them trade papers and attempt to complete the task or find problems/ambiguities with the instructions they receive.

The View From Saturday Lesson Twelve Continued

Discuss:
>Did anyone have any problems writing or following the directions?
>What, if anything, made the composition difficult?
>What, if anything, made following someone else's directions difficult?
>What did you learn from this exercise?
>What advice do you think Tillie would offer us on this topic?

*Homework Create an illustration of a character in the novel–it can be a minor or major character. As an alternative, you may choose to represent--or bring to class--an item that one of the characters might possess. Please do not identify the character or object where the character's name can be seen, since we will be doing an activity with these on (date for Lesson Fourteen).

LESSON THIRTEEN

Objective
   To preview and read Chapters 8-12

Activity
   Give students this class period to preview the study questions, do the vocabulary worksheets for, and read Chapters 8-12.

Read through all the instructions before beginning.

1. Write your first name in the upper right hand corner of this paper.

2. Under your name, write the number of letters your first name contains.

3. Multiply that number times 3.

4. Subtract 2. If the number is less than 15, fold this paper into a paper airplane, put your pencil down, and remain seated. If the number is greater than 15, turn your paper over, put your pencil down and stand beside your chair.

5. Turn your paper over and sit quietly.

6. Only do steps five and six of these instructions.

Read through all the instructions before beginning.

1. Write your first name in the upper right hand corner of this paper.

2. Under your name, write the number of letters your first name contains.

3. Multiply that number times 3.

4. Subtract 2. If the number is less than 15, fold this paper into a paper airplane, put your pencil down, and remain seated. If the number is greater than 15, turn your paper over, put your pencil down and stand beside your chair.

5. Turn your paper over and sit quietly.

6. Only do steps five and six of these instructions

LESSON FOURTEEN

Objectives
1. To review the main events and ideas of Chapters 8-12
2. To examine narrator and point of view in the novel
3. To examine character development from a variety of perspectives
4. To use graphic organizers to study literature
5. To give students an opportunity to analyze characterizations

Activity #1
Tell students to look at their study questions for Chapters 8-12. Discuss the answers in detail and make sure students have the correct answers for study purposes.

Activity #2
Students should complete this activity individually, though you may guide them through each step and answer questions when necessary.

Have each student divide a sheet of paper into three columns.

Go through the novel and list all of the chapter headings in the **first column** (simply put the chapter numbers when the chapters change).

Beside each of these headings, in the **second column**, go back and write who the narrator is and from what point of view the narrator is speaking (*Although it is assumed that your students are familiar with basic points of view, narrators, etc, you may choose to have a quick review or mini-lesson over these terms if you feel it is necessary for your students.*)

In the **third column**, write the setting for that section of the novel. When and where does the action at this point of the story occur?

After everyone has completed this chart, have a discussion about the students responses, allowing them to volunteer their answers and questions. Explain that the structure of this novel is a bit complex, therefore creating a chart can make the structure more clear. Introduce the term **flashback** and explain its relevance to the novel and its pertinence to the point of view and narrative voice in this novel. Subsequently, understanding the characters of the novel becomes essential to understanding the overall structure and themes of the novel. Ask the students: How does this structure highlight the thematic content of the book? (i.e., The Souls, journeys, voice versus silence, balance)

A View From Saturday Lesson Fourteen Continued

Activity #3
    Assign a character/narrator to each student (it is important that several students have the same narrator so that comparisons can be made). First, students should brainstorm characteristics about their characters- physical, emotional, and personal. Next, ask students to look back at the portions of the novel where these characters speak in the first person. What can we tell about them in these sections? Does the character use certain elements repeatedly or a particular style throughout? Would the reader be able to differentiate between the various narrators *without* the narrator being identified, simply by analyzing the narrative style?

NOTE: *If time and interest permit, this could be an interesting experiment: Ask students to identify who is the narrator in several excerpts from the novel–be careful not to give away any factual clues in the excerpt, thereby forcing the students to rely on their comprehension of each character's style and voice.*

    You may have students use a character web as part of this lesson.
    Whole group discussion: Students should share their responses as a class. Are there any disagreements or conflicts among the students in your class? Why? Is there a right answer?

    Pose this question again towards the end of the class discussion:
What is the connection between narrator, point-of-view, and character?

Activity #3 (Remainder of class)
Students should take out their homework assignments from Lesson Twelve. Take turns showing the item to the class; the class should attempt to guess who the character is, or to whom the possession should belong. Find a place to display the items in the classroom.

LESSON FIFTEEN

Objectives
    1. To give students practice writing in the first person point of view
    2. To give students the opportunity to make a connection between themselves and the novel
    3. To give students an opportunity to analyze character motivations in their own writing
    4. To give the teacher an opportunity to evaluate student writing

Activity
Distribute Writing Assignment #2. Discuss the directions in detail and give students ample time to complete the assignment. Collect the papers at the end of the class period.

WRITING ASSIGNMENT #2 *The View from Saturday*

PROMPT
Throughout the novel, Konigsburg shifts the narrative voice as the point of view of the novel changes. As we have discussed, this "flashback" structure is important to all aspects of our "journey" through the novel.

Choose an episode from your own life–a flashback to a time in your childhood or recent past–that you shared with a parent or grandparent. Write about that time, including the circumstances surrounding the experience, your feelings, and descriptions of the other "characters." Make the story come alive for the reader, and attempt to use a style that is recognizably yours. FACT: No one will write the same experience exactly the same way. FACT: You have characteristics that are uniquely yours.

PREWRITING
Brainstorm important moments that you have spent with your parents and/or grandparents. Are there traditions that you share with any of these individuals routinely? Do you share any hobbies or interests? Have you learned any skills from your parents or grandparents that are still prevalent in your life?

If you have difficulty narrowing down a topic, you may choose to make two lists: PARENTS and GRANDPARENTS. From those lists, determine whether one episode stands out more than the others. Do you feel an emotional connection to one of the experiences that you listed, more so than the others?

DRAFTING
Since this is a personal narrative, the style may be less formal than a speech or essay. The writing is a personal record of your thoughts and feelings, so you may adopt a more conversational tone. You will also want to capture your personal narrative voice. If your classmates were to read your essay, would they recognize that you were the author?

You should still have an opening paragraph that introduces yourself and the characters in your narrative, as well as the experience you are describing. Two or three paragraphs should follow the introduction, in which you give the reader insight into the relationship with your family member. You might explain the experiences that the two of you have together, the role the parent or grandparent plays in your life, and your feelings for that individual.

PEER CONFERENCING/REVISING
    When you finish the rough draft of your paper, ask a student who sits near you to read it. After reading your rough draft, he/she should tell you what he/she liked best about your work, which parts were difficult to understand, and ways in which your work could be improved. Reread your paper considering your critic's comments, and make the corrections you think are necessary.

PROOFREADING
    Do a final proofreading of your paper double-checking your grammar, spelling, organization, and the clarity of your ideas.

LESSON SIXTEEN

Objectives
1. To discuss the novel on a deeper than direct recall level
2. To focus on interpretation, critical analysis, and personal response

Activity #1
Choose the questions from the Extra Discussion Questions/Writing Assignments which seem most appropriate for your students. A class discussion of these questions is most effective if students have been given the opportunity to formulate answers to the questions prior to the discussion. To this end, you may either have all the students formulate answers to all the questions, divide your class into groups (maybe using the project groups again) and assign one or more questions to each group, or you could assign one question to each student in your class. The option you choose will make a difference in the amount of class time needed for this activity. The class discussion of these questions is scheduled for the second portion of the class, but could take place on a later day if you would like to give your students more time to prepare their answers.

NOTE: The use of graphic organizers may be helpful to students in preparing their answers. Encourage them to use any diagrams or graphics that they feel are necessary.

Activity #2
Class discussion of the Extra Discussion Questions/Writing Assignments

Note 2: The page numbers after the quotations match the Aladdin Paperback edition.

EXTRA WRITING ASSIGNMENTS/DISCUSSION QUESTIONS *The View from Saturday*

<u>Interpretative</u>
1. What are the major conflicts in the novel? Consider both internal and external conflicts.

2. List the main characters in the novel and describe three signature things about each one.

3. What is the point of view throughout the novel? Does it change?

4. What is the setting of this novel?

5. How long is the actual action of the story?

6. How might the structure of the novel change our perception of the duration and location of the story?

7. Describe Margaret Draper as a principal.

<u>Critical</u>
1. How does the generosity that Noah shows at Century Village inspire further kindness from others throughout the novel?

2. How does Nadia's relationship with her father change throughout the novel? What events bring about these changes?

3. How does Mrs. Olinski influence the plot throughout the novel?

4. What roles do the parents, grandparents, and guardians play in this novel? Compare and contrast the different adults in the novel and note how they influence the younger characters.

5. Why is Julian's ivory monkey important in the novel? What does it symbolize?

6. In what ways are The Souls a team outside of the Academic Quiz Bowl competition?

7. Compare and contrast the commissioner and Mr. Singh.

8. Compare Ethan's and Nadia's family life. How are they different? How are they alike?

9. What does afternoon tea become to each of The Souls?

10. Compare and contrast Margaret Draper with Mrs. Olinski. Include information about their past in your discussion.

The View From Saturday Extra Discussion Questions Page 2

11. Compare and contrast Mrs. Olinski and Nadia.

12. What is Mr. Singh's purpose in the novel? What would the novel lack without his character?

13. What indications do we have that The Souls are somehow connected, even before they realize it themselves?

14. How does the relationship among The Souls and Mrs. Olinski change each of them?

15. At the tea party, what does Ethan do that he normally would not? What do you make of his unusual action? Does Ethan recognize this difference in himself? Explain.

16. When Mrs. Reynolds asks Ethan about his brother Lucas, Ethan immediately becomes silent again. Why do you think this happens?

17. What does the dilemma over the doggie treats tell us about Julian's character?

18. How is the concept of "hybrid" important throughout the novel?

Critical/Personal Response

1. Do you agree with Noah that the residents of Century Village have "retired from useful life?" Cite examples to support your answer.

2. How does point of view affect this novel? Do you think the novel would have been strengthened or weakened if Konigsburg had chosen a different narrative technique?

3. Mr. Singh says that The Souls have all traveled on journeys, through which they have found kindness. Do you agree? Do you think this is the main thing that they all share?

4. How would you explain the title of the novel, *The View from Saturday*.

5. Why do you think Konigsburg chose to structure this novel the way she did? What purpose do the flashbacks serve? What do we gain from the flashbacks and shifting point of view?

6. In what ways would you consider The Souls typical sixth graders? In what ways are they extraordinary?

The View From Saturday Extra Discussion Questions Page 3

Personal Response

1. Do you know of a place like Century Village? Explain.

2. Do you have a favorite journey that you have taken? What was it? Did someone go with you or did you go alone? Discuss.

3. The turtle patrols devote a great deal of time and energy to helping the loggerhead population thrive. Has there been a cause that you have volunteered time or money to support? Was it worth the time and effort? What inspired you to undertake the activity? Discuss.

4. Noah gives away some of his treasured items at the wedding reception, which causes other guests to volunteer their own time and talents to each recipient of a prize. What items in this classroom right now might be offered in the same way?

5. A wedding and afternoon tea feature prominently in this novel. What ceremonies exist in your own culture and family? List and explain religious and non-religious examples.

6. Who is your favorite character? Why? Find a passage from the novel that contains a description of your character or that demonstrates the quality that you most admire.

7. Mrs. Olinski differentiates between mischief and malice in the novel. Describe some situations from your own life, or episodes you have witnessed, and classify them as mischief or malice. What do you consider the major difference between the two?

8. With whom (from the novel) would you most like to be friends?

9. With whom did you most identify?

10. What questions do you still have about the novel?

11. What is your favorite scene, moment, or line from the novel?

QUOTATIONS *The View From Saturday*

1. "To her four sixth graders puberty was something they could spell and define but had yet to experience." (2)

2. "Mother then made a remark about how Western Civilization was in a decline because people of my generation knew how to nitpick but not how to write a B&B letter." (5)

3. "The ballpoint pen has been the biggest single factor in the decline of Western Civilization. It makes the written word cheap, fast, and totally without character." (6)

4. "[Century Village] is like a theme park for old people. Almost everyone who lives there is retired from useful life." (7)

5. "When I told Tillie that six steps seemed a lot to have to do before you begin, she said, 'You must think of those six steps not as preparation for the beginning but as the beginning itself." (10)

6. "He was dressed, brushed, coiffed, and blow-dried not just to be seen but to be looked at." (21)

7. "Jews, half-Jews, and WASPs have nothing to do with diversity, Mrs. Olinski. The Indian does. But we don't call them Indians anymore. We call them Native Americans.
"Not this one," she replied." (23)

8. "For all of his training, Dr. Rohmer would never believe that cripples themselves are a diverse group, and some make jokes." (23)

9. "I concluded that many friendships are born and maintained for purely geographical reasons." (29)

10. "Turtles had brought Grandpa and Margaret together." (31)

11. "I did not know then that when I started sixth grade, I would be living in the state of divorce and New York." (33)

12. "Ginger would not be listed. She is a mixed breed. Like me." (35)

13. "My father hovered with the rest of them and said 'fascinating' twice. Hovering had become his great recreational pastime." (36)

14. "As Margaret was explaining this, I thought about my mother's returning to New York. Her birthday is September 12, and I wondered if her need to return to autumn in New York had anything to do with some switch that had been turned on when she emerged." (39).

15. "Inside me there was a lot of best friendship that no one but Ginger was using." (42)

16. "Like Ethan, my father has a strong taste for silence. Mother always said, 'Your father is not a communicator.'" (48)

The View From Saturday Quotations Page 2

17. "I studied my father...The storm in our private lives had picked him up and put him out of place. Me, too. I, too, had been picked up from one place and set down in another. I, too, had been stranded. We both needed help resettling." (55)

18. "'Yep,' he said. 'And there will be times when you or I will need a lift between switches.'" (57)

19. "There is nothing wrong with Lucas, and that is what is wrong with him." (62)

20. "To *them* farming is a lifestyle not a livelihood." (63)

21. "Sometimes silence is a habit that hurts." (70)

22. "For the first time since I started school–no, even longer than that–for the first time ever, I was looking forward to a party. And I knew that part of the reason I was looking forward to it was because Julian had not made it public." (78)

23. "Julian smiled. 'Not quite,' he said. 'Let us say that I am as American as pizza pie. I did not originate here, but I am here to stay.'" (85)

24. "Had I gained something at Sillington House? Or had I lost something there? The answer was yes." (89)

25. "'Chops,' Julian said, 'is to magic what doing scales is to a chanteuse. Without it you cannot be a magician, with it alone you cannot be an artist.'" (93)

26. "'Ethan Potter. I didn't recognize you.' I believe that she did not recognize him, for the person yelling *Bravo!* was Ethan, The Soul–not Ethan, the silent." (105)

26. "He was an island unto himself, definitely not a team player. Ham Knapp was a leader. Ham Knapp had friends." (121)

27. "Mrs. Olinski had a great tolerance for mischief, but she had no patience for malice. (121)

28. "When people come to tea, they are courteous. She thought, I believe in courtesy. It is the way we avoid hurting people's feelings." (125)

29. "She thought that maybe–just maybe–Western Civilization was in a decline because people did not take time to take tea at four o'clock." (125)

30. "I think you enjoy writing on the blackboard, Mr. Knapp," she said. (129)

31. "The class registered its approval with body language that was the equivalent of silent applause." (129)

32. "For a moment above and below eye level, all four limbs stuck out, and then, just as quickly, all four disappeared. It was quite a balancing act." (131)

The View From Saturday Quotations Page 3

33. "Her team seemed to communicate with a secret stealth language that slipped beneath thought. It took only one warning, and they stopped. Just. Like. That." (133)

34. "Sillington House was its own place." (145)

35. "He also learned to regard each port of call as part of the journey and not as destination. Every voyage begins when you do." (151)

36. "And the Souls and Mrs. Olinski shared the trophy that is called a loving cup. And it was." (154)

37. "'For many months now, you have been in a state of perpetual preparation and excitement. Each victory was a preparation for the next. You are missing future victories. Have you enjoyed the journey out, Mrs. Olinski?" (155)

38. "You must know of something's existence before you can notice its absence." (157)

39. "She waited until they were all in their usual places, and then she asked, 'Did I choose you, or did you choose me?"
And The Souls answered, "Yes!" (160)

LESSON SEVENTEEN

Objective
    To review all of the vocabulary work done in this unit

Activity
    Choose one (or more) of the vocabulary review activities listed below and spend your class period as directed in the activity. Some of the materials for these review activities are located in the Vocabulary Resource Materials section in this LitPlan.

VOCABULARY REVIEW ACTIVITIES

1. Divide your class into two teams and have an old-fashioned spelling or definition bee.

2. Give each of your students (or students in groups of two, three or four) an *The View from Saturday* Vocabulary Word Search Puzzle. The person (group) to find all of the vocabulary words in the puzzle first wins.

3. Give students an *The View from Saturday* Vocabulary Word Search Puzzle without the word list. The person or group to find the most vocabulary words in the puzzle wins.

4. Use an *The View from Saturday* Vocabulary Crossword Puzzle. Put the puzzle onto a transparency on the overhead projector (so everyone can see it), and do the puzzle together as a class.

5. Give students an *The View from Saturday* Vocabulary Matching Worksheet to do.

6. Divide your class into two teams. Use *The View from Saturday* vocabulary words with their letters jumbled as a word list. Student 1 from Team A faces off against Student 1 from Team B. You write the first jumbled word on the board. The first student (1A or 1B) to unscramble the word wins the chance for his/her team to score points. If 1A wins the jumble, go to student 2A and give him/her a definition. He/she must give you the correct spelling of the vocabulary word which fits that definition. If he/she does, Team A scores a point, and you give student 3A a definition for which you expect a correctly spelled matching vocabulary word. Continue giving Team A definitions until some team member makes an incorrect response. An incorrect response sends the game back to the jumbled-word face off, this time with students 2A and 2B. Instead of repeating giving definitions to the first few students of each team, continue with the student after the one who gave the last incorrect response on the team. For example, if Team B wins the jumbled-word face-off, and student 5B gave the last incorrect answer for Team B, you would start this round of definition questions with student 6B, and so on. The team with the most points wins!

7. Have students write a story in which they correctly use as many vocabulary words as possible. Have students read their compositions orally! Post the most original compositions on your bulletin board!

LESSON EIGHTEEN

Objectives
1. To broaden students' knowledge on a variety of topics
2. To allow students to practice public speaking skills
3. To allow students to interact to compose a final group project
4. To allow students to determine how their project fits into a larger unit of study

Activity
Choose one of the groups to go first with their group presentations, or allow groups to volunteer. Each group should begin by offering an overview of the topic and presenting the final project. Following each presentation, the class should have an opportunity to ask questions to the group.

NOTE: This may take more than one class period, depending on how involved the projects are.

Follow-up
If you choose, and if time allows, you may follow up the presentations with a discussion of the projects as a whole:

Compare/contrast the class experiences with the experiences portrayed in the novel. Brainstorm and discuss responses as time and interest permit:

What did you learn through the completion of the group project?
Did you meet any new people, share your talents, become involved in a cause that might otherwise have passed you by?
What was your journey like?
How was our journey different from the characters' journeys in the novel?
Did you find kindness along your way?

LESSON NINETEEN

Objectives
1. To define the term "allusion" and its various types
2. To demonstrate how an author's use of allusion contributes to a work's theme development
3. To allow students to explore the development of allusion in other works they have studied
4. To allow students to examine the quality of literature and define criteria for evaluating literature and writing

Activity #1

Write the word "allusion" on the board. Give students an opportunity to define what this word means. Explain that:

In literature, an allusion is a reference to a famous person, place, thing, piece of literature, art, music, etc., that the reader is expected to recognize.

Ask students to provide examples of allusions they have encountered in previous literature study. What allusions can we find in our everyday world? (For example, mythological allusions abound, such as Ajax cleanser and King Triton from Disney's *The Little Mermaid*) Allow the class to brainstorm as many allusions, from as many different sources, as they can.

TRANSITION: In *The View from Saturday*, Konigsburg uses many allusions. How many can you recall without looking back at the text? (List these on the board or overhead) Now, break into your project groups and look through the novel, making a list of any other allusions you find. If you are familiar with the allusion, go ahead and explain its significance in the novel and cite the page number. Otherwise, simply write the page number where you find the reference. *(A list of allusions, complete with page numbers follows this lesson. Though it may not be exhaustive, it contains many of the important allusions in the novel).*

Activity #2

Bring the class back together for whole class discussion. Have the groups form a master list of the allusions they found, and allow the students to explain as many of the references as they can. Highlight any references that the class as a whole is unfamiliar with.

Note: It might be useful to bring examples of as many of the allusions to class as possible, since it will be difficult to determine which topics the students will be familiar with, and which they will not. Following the discussion, circulate the samples that you have brought so the students can have a visual representation.

The View From Saturday Lesson Nineteen Continued

Activity #3
    If possible, get enough copies of *Alice in Wonderland* and *Through the Looking Glass* for every student to have a copy. Spend some time looking through the illustrations in both works and discussing the literature in an open format. Why might Konigsburg have chosen this particular piece of literature to reference in her piece? Consider all the ways the two Carroll novels are used in *The View From Saturday*. What impact would another choice have had on *View*? What does the breadth and variety of the allusions used tell us about Konigsburg? What does your class think about her as a **writer**? How does she compare with other **writers** they have studied? What criteria should we use to determine **good literature**? Does it matter? What should be the ultimate determination of whether a book is used in a classroom? Do you think *View* is a good choice?

Note: If time or interest permit, you may choose to extend this discussion, or show some of the videos recommended in the Extra Resources portion of this LitPlan (#9 in More Activities).

Also Note that the page numbers in the List of Allusions match the Aladdin Paperback edition.

LIST OF ALLUSIONS *The View From Saturday*

Alice in Wonderland /Through the Looking Glass(literature)
by Lewis Carroll
    p. 22
    pp. 76-77
    p. 158

Raphael/cherubs (art)
    p. 23

Jack Sprat (literature/nursery rhyme)
    p. 27

Phantom of the Opera (music/theater)
    p. 40

The Arabian Nights (literature)
    p. 65

water lilies (art)
    p. 80

Annie/Sandy (music/theater)

    p. 99
"Little Orphan Annie" comic strip
    p. 100

David and Goliath/slingshots (biblical)
    p. 128

Hecate's soul
    p. 143

National Geographic cameraman
    p. 36

Waterloo (historical)
    pp. 137-138

First Amendment to the Constitutions
    p. 120

See questions listed at end of novel for other possibilities

LESSON TWENTY

<u>Objectives</u>
    1. To give students the opportunity to practice writing to persuade
    2. To encourage students' critical thinking skills
    3. To have students explore a real-life connection to *The View from Saturday*
    4. To give the teacher the opportunity to evaluate students' writing skills
    5. To give students the opportunity to write and perform a speech

<u>Activity</u>
    Distribute Writing Assignment #3. Discuss the directions in detail and give students ample time to complete the assignment. While students are writing, call individual students to your desk or some other private area for a writing conference based on the first two writing assignments in this unit. An evaluation form is included in this unit for your convenience.

WRITING ASSIGNMENT #3 - *The View from Saturday*

PROMPT

"Mother then made a remark about how Western Civilization was in a decline because people of my generation knew how to nitpick but not how to write a B&B letter." (5)

"The ballpoint pen has been the biggest single factor in the decline of Western Civilization. It makes the written word cheap, fast, and totally without character." (6)

"She thought that maybe–just maybe–Western Civilization was in a decline because people did not take time to take tea at four o'clock." (125)

At several points in the novel, characters offer reasons for the "Decline of Western Civilization." What do you think is a likely cause of the present-day's decline–or is Western Civilization indeed on the decline? Write a speech to be presented to your classmates in which you highlight the cause of the current decline, the reasons your peers should be concerned about these facts, and how the decline might be halted.

PREWRITING

First you must consider your audience and your argument. List problems that you think might have caused a decline in modern civilization. Why is this problem so harmful? How might the regression be improved? Cite evidence and examples whenever possible to strengthen your argument. You must also explain to your peers why this issue affects them, and how they might have the power to prevent any further damage from occurring.

DRAFTING

Remember that this is a speech, not a written essay, so you want to be as dynamic as possible. You must draw your listener in from the first word. Use the techniques you have learned for speech-writing. Begin by clearly stating what the problem is and how it is hurting us. Be clear and use examples. Make sure the audience realizes throughout the speech that this IS a major problem, and it IS important to come up with a solution, and it IS within their power to do so.

PEER CONFERENCING/REVISING

When you finish the rough draft of your paper, ask a student who sits near you to read it. After reading your rough draft, he/she should tell you what he/she liked best about your work, which parts were difficult to understand, and ways in which your work could be improved. Reread your paper considering your critic's comments, and make the corrections you think are necessary.

PROOFREADING

Do a final proofreading of your paper double-checking your grammar, spelling, organization, and the clarity of your ideas.

WRITING EVALUATION FORM - *The View from Saturday*

Name _____ Date _____

Grade _____

Circle One For Each Item:

Grammar:	correct	errors noted on paper
Spelling:	correct	errors noted on paper
Punctuation:	correct	errors noted on paper
Legibility:	excellent	good fair poor
_____	excellent	good fair poor
_____	excellent	good fair poor

Strengths:

Weaknesses:

Comments/Suggestions:

LESSON TWENTY-ONE

Objective
To review the main ideas and events in *The View from Saturday*

Activity (Entire class)
Choose one of the review games/activities suggested in this unit and spend your class time as directed there. Conducting an Academic Quiz Bowl as review would be particularly appropriate for this unit. You could choose teams from one class, or combine classes for a special review day. You might combine questions from the novel, as well as the questions the students' developed as a part of their Group Projects.

REVIEW GAMES/ACTIVITIES *The View from Saturday*

1. Ask the class to make up a unit test for *The View from Saturday*. The test should have 4 sections: matching, true/false, short answer, and essay. Students may use 1/2 period to make the test and then swap papers and use the other 1/2 class period to take a test a classmate has devised. (open book) You may want to use the unit test included in this packet or take questions from the students' unit tests to formulate your own test.

2. Take 1/2 period for students to make up true and false questions (including the answers). Collect the papers and divide the class into two teams. Draw a big tic-tac-toe board on the chalk board. Make one team X and one team O. Ask questions to each side, giving each student one turn. If the question is answered correctly, that students' team's letter (X or O) is placed in the box. If the answer is incorrect, no letter is placed in the box. The object is to get three in a row like tic-tac-toe. You may want to keep track of the number of games won for each team.

3. Take 1/2 period for students to make up questions (true/false and short answer). Collect the questions. Divide the class into two teams. You'll alternate asking questions to individual members of teams A & B (like in a spelling bee). The question keeps going from A to B until it is correctly answered, then a new question is asked. A correct answer does not allow the team to get another question. Correct answers are +2 points; incorrect answers are -1 point.

4. Have students pair up and quiz each other from their study guides and class notes.

5. Give students an *The View from Saturday* crossword puzzle to complete.

6. Divide your class into two teams. Use *The View from Saturday* crossword words with their letters jumbled as a word list. Student 1 from Team A faces off against Student 1 from Team B. You write the first jumbled word on the board. The first student (1A or 1B) to unscramble the word wins the chance for his/her team to score points. If 1A wins the jumble, go to student 2A and give him/her a clue. He/she must give you the correct word which matches that clue. If he/she does, Team A scores a point, and you give student 3A a clue for which you expect another correct response. Continue giving Team A clues until some team member makes an

incorrect response. An incorrect response sends the game back to the jumbled-word face off, this time with students 2A and 2B. Instead of repeating giving clues to the first few students of each team, continue with the student after the one who gave the last incorrect response on the team. For example, if Team B wins the jumbled-word face-off, and student 5B gave the last incorrect answer for Team B, you would start this round of clue questions with student 6B, and so on. The team with the most points wins!

8. Play What's My Line?. This is similar to the old television show. Students assume the roles of different characters from the epic. One student gives clues to the class, or to a panel of contestants. The contestants try to guess the identity of the guest. Students may enjoy assisting you in creating rules and procedures for the game.

9. Play Jeopardy. Divide the class into two groups. Assign each group a category or book from the epic and have them devise answers for that category. Play the game according to the television show procedures.

10. Play Drawing in the Details. This is similar to Pictionary. Divide students into teams. A student from one team draws a scene from the epic. (You may want to specify the Book or section.) Drawings should be kept simple, to keep the pace lively. Students in the opposing team locate the scene in their books and read it aloud. If they are incorrect, the illustrator's team has a chance to guess. Involve students in setting up a scoring system and any other necessary rules.

UNIT TESTS

SHORT ANSWER UNIT TEST 1 - *The View from Saturday*

I. Matching/Identify

____ 1. allusion   A. Town where The Souls live

____ 2. calligraphy   B. In literature, a reference to a famous person, place, or artistic work that the reader is expected to recognize

____ 3. *zatfig*   C. Julian's toy that symbolizes balance

____ 4. chops   D. Decorative handwriting

____ 5. paraplegic   E. Retirement community

____ 6. suburbanites   F. People who live in outlying residential areas of a city

____ 7. hybrid   G. Author of *Alice in Wonderland* and *Through the Looking Glass*

____ 8. Century Village   H. Internal mechanism that leads turtles where they need to go at various stages in their lives

____ 9. Epiphany   I. Pen points

____ 10. Lewis Carroll   J. A person whose legs and lower body are paralyzed

____ 11. nibs   K. Slight-of-hand technique that is basis for magic

____ 12. switch   L. Pleasingly plump

____ 13. Sargasso Sea   M. The product of two different varieties or species

____ 14. Raphael   N. Annie's best friend

____ 15. halos   O. SONAR, POSH, TIP

____ 16. loggerheads   P. Famous artist, known for his paintings of cherubs

____ 17. Sandy   Q. Portion of North Atlantic Ocean where much marine life thrives

____ 18. ivory monkey   R. Threatened turtle species

____ 19. Humpty Dumpty   S. Well-known figure from *Through the Looking Glass*

____ 20. acronyms   T. Ethan appreciates these

The View from Saturday Short Answer Unit Test 1 Page 2

II. Short Answer

1. What is a B & B letter? Who wrote one, to whom, and for what?

2. What is Century Village? Who lives there?

3. Why does Nadia call herself a mixed breed?

4. Where did Margaret live before moving to Florida?

5. What brought Margaret and Izzy together?

6. Why did Mrs. Olinski leave teaching?

7. What are Ethan's dreams for the future?

8. What are the Singhs' plans for Sillington house?

9. Why was Mrs. Olinski reluctant to choose Julian for her team?

The View from Saturday Short Answer Unit Test 1 Page 3

10. Who does Mrs. Olinski ask for an explanation regarding her choices for the quiz bowl team, and what is his explanation?

11. What have all of The Souls found?

12. Who gives The Souls their name? Why did that person get to pick the name?

13. What question does Mrs. Olinski ask the group when they are seated inside Sillington House, and what is their response?

14. What two books does Mr.s Olinski look at just before going to bed after Bowl Day?

The View from Saturday Short Answer Unit Test 1 Page 4
III. Essay

Why is Silllington House important in the novel? Do the experiences at Silington House affect the characters' experiences in the larger world? What does the house represent for the characters in the novel? Choose 4 characters for your discussion.

IV. Vocabulary
   Write down the vocabulary words. Go back later and write down the correct definition for each word.

1.

2.

3.

4.

5.

6.

7.

8.

9.

10.

SHORT ANSWER UNIT TEST 1 ANSWER KEY - *The View from Saturday*

I. Matching/Identify
1. B
2. D
3. L
4. K
5. J
6. F
7. M
8. E
9. A
10. G
11. I
12. H
13. Q
14. P
15. T
16. R
17. N
18. C
19. S
20. O

II. Short Answer

1. What is a B & B letter? Who wrote one, to whom, and for what?
    A B & B letter is a "bread and butter" letter, a thank-you note. Noah wrote one to his grandparents thanking them for his nice visit and the gifts he received while he was visiting.

2. What is Century Village? Who lives there?
    Century Village is a retirement community. Noah's grandmother (Margaret Draper) and Nadia's grandfather (Izzy Diamondstein), who recently got married, live there.

3. Why does Nadia call herself a mixed breed?
    She is half-Jewish and half-Protestant.

4. Where did Margaret live before moving to Florida?
    She lived in Epiphany, New York, the home town of The Souls.

5. What brought Margaret and Izzy together?
    Turtles brought them together.

6. Why did Mrs. Olinski leave teaching?
    She left teaching when she had a terrible automobile accident that left her a widow and a paraplegic.

7. What are Ethan's dreams for the future?
    Ethan wants to design costumes or sets for the theater.

8. What are the Singhs' plans for Sillington house?
    They plan to turn it into a bed and breakfast inn.

9. Why was Mrs. Olinski reluctant to choose Julian for her team?
    She thought Julian was a loner, not a team player.

10. Who does Mrs. Olinski ask for an explanation regarding her choices for the quiz bowl team, and what is his explanation?
    Mrs. Olinski asks Mr. Singh, who explains that each of The Souls have returned from a journey.

11. What have all of The Souls found?
    They have found kindness.

12. Who gives The Souls their name? Why did that person get to pick the name?
    Nadia pulled off the biggest strip of wallpaper and won the right to pick the name. She chose The Souls.

13. What question does Mrs. Olinski ask the group when they are seated inside Sillington House, and what is their response?
    She asks them if she chose them or if they chose her. Their response is, "Yes!"

14. What two books does Mr.s Olinski look at just before going to bed after Bowl Day?
    She looks at *Alice in Wonderland* and *Through the Looking Glass*.

SHORT ANSWER UNIT TEST 2 - *The View from Saturday*

I. Matching/Identify

____ 1. allusion	A. Ethan appreciates these

____ 2. calligraphy	B. Well-known figure from *Through the Looking Glass*

____ 3. *zatfig*	C. Threatened turtle species

____ 4. chops	D. Portion of North Atlantic Ocean where much marine life thrives

____ 5. paraplegic	E. famous artist, known for his paintings of cherubs

____ 6. suburbanites	F. SONAR, POSH, TIP

____ 7. hybrid	G. Annie's best friend

____ 8. Century Village	H. The product of two different varieties or species

____ 9. Epiphany	I. Julian's toy that symbolizes balance

____ 10. Lewis Carroll	J. Slight-of-hand technique that is basis for magic

____ 11. nibs	K. A person whose legs and lower body are paralyzed

____ 12. switch	L. Pen points

____ 13. Sargasso Sea	M. Internal mechanism that leads turtles where they need to go at various stages in their lives

____ 14. Raphael	N. Author of *Alice in Wonderland* and *Through the Looking Glass*

____ 15. halos	O. People who live in outlying residential areas of a city

____ 16. loggerheads	P. Retirement community

____ 17. Sandy	Q. Decorative handwriting

____ 18. ivory monkey	R. Pleasingly plump

____ 19. Humpty Dumpty	S. In literature, a reference to a famous person, place, or artistic work that the reader is expected to recognize

____ 20. acronyms	T. Town where The Souls live

The View from Saturday Short Answer Unit Test 2 Page 2

II. Short Answer

1. Who selects the team for the Academic Bowl, and how does she do it differently from most in her position?

2. What is extraordinary about The Souls?

3. What skill does Noah learn from Tillie Nachman, and to whom does he teach it?

4. What were the specially marked invitations?

5. How does Nadia react to Ethan's disclosing things he knows about her life?

6. How do Julian and Ethan first and continually meet other than as a part of The Souls?

7. What decision did Julian have to make about the doggie treats? What does he do?

8. What is Dr. Rohmer concerned about before the competition?

The View from Saturday Short Answer Unit Test 2 Page 3

9. Describe Julian's personality.

10. How does Mrs. Olinski know Margaret Draper?

11. Who is Margaret Draper to Ethan?

12. How is Nadia connected to Margaret Draper? Does Nadia like Margaret?

13. How is Nadia "connected" to Noah Gershom?

14. What event(s) do The Souls look forward to at Sillington House?

The View from Saturday Short Answer Unit Test 2 Page 4

III. Composition

Mr. Singh explains to Mrs. Olinski that each of The Souls has returned from a journey. Describe the journey that each of The Souls undertakes, and explain how it prepareed them for Epiphany Middle School. Do you think Mrs. Olinski's home room is the destination? Explain your answer.

The View from Saturday Short Answer Unit Test 2 Page 5

IV. Vocabulary

Write down the vocabulary words. Go back later and write down the correct definitions for the words.

1.

2.

3.

4.

5.

6.

7.

8.

9.

10.

ANSWER KEY: SHORT ANSWER UNIT TEST 2 - *The View from Saturday*

I. Matching/Identify
- 1. S
- 2. Q
- 3. R
- 4. J
- 5. K
- 6. O
- 7. H
- 8. P
- 9. T
- 10. N
- 11. L
- 12. M
- 13. D
- 14. E
- 15. A
- 16. C
- 17. G
- 18. I
- 19. B
- 20. F

II Short Answer

1. Who selects the team for the Academic Bowl, and how does she do it differently from most in her position?
    Mrs. Olinski selects the team members by appointment rather than by try-outs.

2. What is extraordinary about The Souls?
    They make it to the championships even though they are all sixth graders.

3. What skill does Noah learn from Tillie Nachman, and to whom does he teach it?
    Noah learns calligraphy and teaches The Souls about it.

4. What were the specially marked invitations?
    They were invitations to the wedding with the cat's paw prints. Rather than making new invitations, the group decided to award prizes to the recipients by covering the paw prints with marked post-it notes.

5. How does Nadia react to Ethan's disclosing things he knows about her life?
    She is furious that he knows things about her life that she doesn't.

6. How do Julian and Ethan first and continually meet other than as a part of The Souls?
    Julian sits with Ethan on the school bus.

7. What decision did Julian have to make about the doggie treats? What does he do?
    Julian had to decide whether or not to substitute back the good treats for the ones that had been tampered with. He replaces the harmful treats with the good ones.

8. What is Dr. Rohmer concerned about before the competition?
    He is worried about his contract renewal, the district playoffs, and how Fairbain's performance might affect them.

9. Describe Julian's personality.
    He doesn't fit in with the Epiphany School kids at first because he comes from a different background. He dresses and speaks very differently from the other kids. But he is smart– smart enough to be himself and to do things that intrigue the other kids, showing them that being different isn't necessarily a bad thing.

10. How does Mrs. Olinski know Margaret Draper?
    Margaret Draper was the principal at a school where Mrs. Olinksi used to teach.

11. Who is Margaret Draper to Ethan?
    She is his grandmother.

12. How is Nadia connected to Margaret Draper? Does Nadia like Margaret?
    Nadia's grandfather Izzy married Margaret. Nadia does not like Margaret.

13. How is Nadia "connected" to Noah Gershom?
    Nadia's mother works for Noah's father.

14. What event(s) do The Souls look forward to at Sillington House?
    They look forward to 4 o'clock tea.

MULTIPLE CHOICE UNIT TEST 1 - *The View from Saturday*

I. Matching

____ 1. AUGUST   A. Izzy's wife; Ethan's grandmother; former principal

____ 2. LUCAS   B. Portion of the North Atlantic where marine life thrives: ___ Sea

____ 3. KORSHAK   C. Master of Ceremonies at the district playoffs

____ 4. SINGH   D. Nadia spends this month with her father.

____ 5. FAIRBAIN   E. Nadia takes this gift to the first tea party

____ 6. CALLIGRAPHY F. Village where Margaret and Izzy live

____ 7. TREATS   G. Tea party location: ___ House

____ 8. GINGER   H. Margaret's grandson

____ 9. MAXWELL   I. The Souls attended ___ Middle School.

____10. EPIPHANY   J. Noah used his red one to transport things to the clubhouse.

____11. PAW   K. Bus driver for Epiphany

____12. SARGASSO   L. Noah teaches this skill to The Souls.

____13. PUZZLE   M. Epiphany competes against this school on Bowl Day.

____14. CENTURY   N. Kind of prints on the wedding invitations

____15. DIAMONDSTEIN O. Izzy's last name

____16. KNAPP   P. Julian's toy symbolizing balance: ivory ___

____17. MARGARET   Q. State where Nadia's father lives

____18. MICHAEL   R. Julian's last name

____19. SILLINGTON   S. Nadia's dog

____20. PUPPY   T. Ham laced Ginger's with tranquilizers and laxatives

____21. MONKEY   U. Ham's last name

____22. ETHAN   V. Arnold's owner

____23. FLORIDA   W. Gift Ethan takes to the first tea party

____24. WAGON   X. Julian magically placed one in the hand of each of The Souls.

____25. PENNY   Y. Ethan's older, perfect brother

The View from Saturday Multiple Choice Unit Test 1 Page 2

II. Multiple Choice

1. What is "extraordinary" about The Souls?
    A. They are quadruplets.
    B. They speak 12 languages among them.
    C. They make it to the state championship as sixth graders.
    D. They are also champion racquetball players.
2. To whom must Noah write a B&B letter?
    A. Sillington House
    B. His grandparents at Century Village
    C. Allen Diamondstein
    D. Mrs. Olinski
3. Who gets married at Century Village?
    A. The governor of Florida
    B. The owner of Century Village
    C. Noah's parents
    D. Margaret Draper and Izzy Diamondstein
4. What are the "specially-marked invitations?"
    A. Invitations marked with a paw print and post-it note
    B. Invitations for guests who sit on the front row
    C. Invitations for the family members of the bride and groom
    D. Invitations for guests who wanted to be photographed
5. What brings Margaret and Izzy together?
    A. Allen
    B. Turtles
    C. Ballroom dance classes
    D. A mutual love for Zora Neale Hurston novels
6. Why doesn't Mrs. Olinski tell Ethan that she knew his grandmother?
    A. She is ashamed.
    B. She wants to discover Ethan for herself.
    C. She knows Ethan does not speak to his grandmother.
    D. She doesn't realize Ethan is Margaret's grandson.
7. How does Ethan describe his older brother Lucas?
    A. He's "Angry and withdrawn."
    B. He's "Young and whiny."
    C. There's "nothing wrong with him, and that's what's wrong with him."
    D. He's "Completely forgettable."

The View from Saturday Multiple Choice Unit Test 1 Page 3

8. What are the Singhs' plans for Sillington house?
   - A. Tear it down to build a new home
   - B. Turn it into a bed and breakfast
   - C. Turn it into an orphanage
   - D. Turn it into a dentist office
9. What object does Julian show to The Souls at their weekly tea?
   - A. A red ball
   - B. A cruise ship
   - C. An ivory monkey
   - D. A book
10. What does Julian overhear Ham Knapp discussing during the ride to the matinee?
    - A. His love for *Annie*
    - B. His parents' new home
    - C. His plan to tranquilize Ginger
    - D. His mother's new cat
11. Why does Mrs. Olinski call Julian aside following the performance?
    - A. She thinks he spiked the treats.
    - B. She knows he was getting Ginger ready.
    - C. She wants to know where Nadia is.
    - D. She wants to give Julian a ride to Sillington House.
12. What unusual thing does Mrs. Olinski observe about the four sixth graders at Sillington House?
    - A. They are courteous and polite with one another.
    - B. They always dress alike.
    - C. They all have the same middle name.
    - D. They sing beautifully together.
13. How does the team respond to Julian's defiance of the commissioner?
    - A. They are horrified.
    - B. They apologize.
    - C. They support him.
    - D. They pretend not to know him.
14. Why does Dr. Rohmer feel this year's competition will draw a larger audience?
    - A. It's televised.
    - B. A new library will be built at the winning school.
    - C. It's the final year the competition will be held.
    - D. Everyone wants to see Homer Fairbain make mistakes.
15. Why do The Souls decline a Saturday practice at the school?
    - A. They are tired of practicing.
    - B. They are going to be out of town.
    - C. They have tea every Saturday.
    - D. They are quitting the team.

The View from Saturday Multiple Choice Unit Test 1 Page 4

16. How does Mr. Singh make Mrs. Olinski uneasy?
    A. He asks her on a date.
    B. He knows things about her selection of the team that she has not told anyone.
    C. He asks for her resignation.
    D. He asks about her disability.
17. Why does the commissioner of education penalize Julian?
    A. For telling Nadia the answer
    B. For challenging the panel's decision
    C. For leaving in the middle of the competition
    D. For calling the other team names
18. Which two books did Mrs. Olinski look at just before going to bed after Bowl Day?
    A. *The Bible* and her personal journal
    B. *Alice in Wonderland* and *Through the Looking Glass*
    C. *A Tale of Two Cities* and *Oliver Twist*
    D. *A Midsummer Night's Dream* and *Much Ado About Nothing*
19. What question does Mrs. Olinski ask The Souls when they are seated at their final meeting at Sillington House?
    A. "Can I have a sandwich?"
    B. "Cream or sugar?"
    C. "Did I choose you, or did you choose me?"
    D. "How are you?"

The View from Saturday Multiple Choice Unit Test 1 Page 5

III. Composition

1. How does the generosity that Noah shows at Century Village inspire further kindness from others throughout the novel?

2. List the main characters in the novel and describe three signature things about each one.

3. Why is Julian's ivory monkey important in the novel? What does it symbolize?

4. In what ways are The Souls a team outside of the Academic Quiz Bowl competition?

The View from Saturday Multiple Choice Unit Test 1 Page 6

IV. Vocabulary - Match the correct definitions to the words.

____ 1. SUPPRESSED   A. Compact and succinct
____ 2. REFRAINED   B. Came from different directions toward a central point
____ 3. VULGAR   C. Behaving as if one has complete rule over others
____ 4. TRANSLUCENCE   D. Extremely badly
____ 5. IRONIC   E. Continuing without change or end
____ 6. ATROCIOUSLY   F. Podium
____ 7. LECTERN   G. Able to cut into fourths
____ 8. PRETEXT   H. False excuse
____ 9. QUARTERING   I. In biology, a category above species and below family
____ 10. MEDIOCRE   J. Inattention
____ 11. NEGLECT   K. Decided through reasoning and deliberation
____ 12. JUBILANT   L. Occurring in a manner opposite to what is expected
____ 13. CONVERGED   M. Charmingly old-fashioned
____ 14. CAPSULE   N. Average to below average in quality
____ 15. INEVITABLE   O. Lively
____ 16. SENTINELS   P. Certain; with an unavoidable outcome
____ 17. ORIGINATE   Q. Kindly
____ 18. QUAINT   R. Guards
____ 19. CONCLUDED   S. Have a beginning
____ 20. ANIMATED   T. Without relaxation or distraction
____ 21. GENUS   U. Lacking charm, culture, or sophistication
____ 22. STRICT   V. Prevented from being expressed; kept down
____ 23. PERPETUAL   W. Triumphantly happy
____ 24. BENEVOLENTLY   X. State of being semi-transparent
____ 25. DICTATORIAL   Y. Kept oneself from doing something

MULTIPLE CHOICE UNIT TEST 2 - *The View from Saturday*

I. Matching

____ 1. PENNY　　　　　　　A. Kind of prints on the wedding invitations

____ 2. NOAH　　　　　　　B. Grade level of the Academic Bowl team students

____ 3. IZZY　　　　　　　　C. Arnold's owner

____ 4. DIAMONDSTEIN　　D. State where Nadia's father lives

____ 5. MICHAEL　　　　　E. Portion of the North Atlantic where marine life thrives: ___ Sea

____ 6. DRAPER　　　　　　F. Epiphany competes against this school on Bowl Day.

____ 7. WAGON　　　　　　G. Izzy's last name

____ 8. OPERA　　　　　　　H. Noah used his red one to transport things to the clubhouse.

____ 9. FLORIDA　　　　　　I. Master of Ceremonies at the district playoffs

____10. POTTER　　　　　　J. Margaret's last name before marrying Izzy

____11. LUCAS　　　　　　　K. Ethan really enjoyed this performance: Phantom of the ___

____12. GERSHOM　　　　　L. Ginger's stage role

____13. SIXTH　　　　　　　M. Term meaning pleasingly plump

____14. HOVERING　　　　　N. Ham's last name

____15. ZATFIG　　　　　　　O. Dr. __: Noah's father; Nadia's mother works for him

____16. FAIRBAIN　　　　　　P. Nadia's father's new best thing

____17. LETTER　　　　　　　Q. B & B: a kind of ____ Noah had to write

____18. PARAPLEGIC　　　　R. Ethan's older, perfect brother

____19. SANDY　　　　　　　S. Best man at the wedding

____20. KNAPP　　　　　　　T. Julian magically placed one in the hand of each of The Souls.

____21. ROHMER　　　　　　U. The Souls found this on their journey.

____22. MAXWELL　　　　　V. District Superintendent of Clarion County

____23. KINDNESS　　　　　W. Ethan or Lucas

____24. SARGASSO　　　　　X. Margaret's husband; Nadia's grandfather

____25. PAW　　　　　　　　Y. Word describing Mrs. Olinski's physical condition

View From Saturday Multiple Choice Unit Test 2 Page 2

II. Multiple Choice

1. What brings Margaret and Izzy together?
    A. Allen
    B. A mutual love for Zora Neal Hurston novels
    C. Ballroom dance classes
    D. Turtles
2. What reason does Nadia's mother give for moving back to New York?
    A. She misses the autumn
    B. She finds a job there
    C. She cannot afford to live in Florida
    D. Her family is in New York
3. What are Ethan's dreams for the future?
    A. To go in business with Lucas
    B. To take over the family farm
    C. To become a dentist
    D. To become a costume/set designer
4. Where did Margaret live before moving to Florida?
    A. Charlottesville, VA
    B. Washington, DC
    C. Epiphany, NY
    D. Los Angeles, CA
5. What is a B & B letter?
    A. A note of apology
    B. A note mailed on the bed and breakfast inn letterhead
    C. A request for reservations at a bed and breakfast inn
    D. A thank-you note
6. Why did Mrs. Olinski leave teaching?
    A. She was in a car accident
    B. She wanted to pursue a different career
    C. She gave birth to her first child
    D. She moved to Europe
7. Why does Nadia call herself a mixed breed?
    A. Because her pet is not pure-bred
    B. Because she is half-Jewish and half-Protestant
    C. Because she loves winter and summer
    D. Because she likes both country and rock-and-roll music

The View from Saturday Multiple Choice Unit Test 2 Page 3

8. What is Nadia's dog's name?
   A. Arnold
   B. Sandy
   C. Ginger
   D. Froelich
9. What is Century Village?
   A. A retirement community
   B. A futuristic representation of the world in 2100
   C. An historic town founded in south Florida in 1800
   D. A shopping district
10. What unusual physical characteristic does Mrs. Olinski discuss with her class on the first day of school?
    A. Albinoism
    B. Green Hair
    C. Paraplegia
    D. Orange skin
11. What physical characteristic does Ethan most admire about Nadia?
    A. Eyes
    B. Hands
    C. Legs
    D. Halo hair
12. Why was Mrs. Olinski reluctant to choose Julian for her team?
    A. She thought he was lazy
    B. She thought he was moving away
    C. She didn't think he would work well on a team
    D. She wanted to choose a girl
13. What are the Singhs' plans for Sillington house?
    A. Tear it down to build a new home
    B. Turn it into a bed and breakfast
    C. Turn it into an orphanage
    D. Turn it into a dentist office
14. Who does Mrs. Olinski ask for an explanation regarding her choices for the quiz bowl team?
    A. The Souls
    B. Mrs. Gershom
    C. Julian
    D. Mr. Singh

The View from Saturday Multiple Choice Unit Test 2 Page 4

15. What is the explanation regarding Mrs. Olinski's team member choices?
    A. They have all been on a journey.
    B. They were the smartest in her class.
    C. It was random chance.
    D. He has no explanation.
16. Who gives The Souls their name?
    A. Julian
    B. Nadia
    C. Mrs. Olinski
    D. Margaret Draper
17. What have all of The Souls found?
    A. Kindness
    B. A talent
    C. Tea
    D. A pet
18. Who rides with Mrs. Olinski to the competition in Albany?
    A. Ginger
    B. Nadia
    C. Margaret Diamondstein
    D. The Singhs

The View from Saturday Multiple Choice Unit Test 2 Page 5

III. Composition

1. Compare and contrast Mrs. Olinski and Nadia.

2. What is Mr. Singh's purpose in the novel? What would the novel lack without his character?

3. Compare and contrast Margaret Draper with Mrs. Olinski.

4. How does the generosity that Noah shows at Century Village inspire further kindness from others throughout the novel?

The View from Saturday Multiple Choice Unit Test 2 Page 5

IV. Vocabulary

____ 1. ANIMATED A. Behaving as if one has complete rule over others

____ 2. PREOCCUPIED B. Strengthen

____ 3. KNOLL C. Method or instinct an animal has for finding its way

____ 4. REINFORCE D. Combining in such a way as to enhance each other

____ 5. INVENTORY E. Reconsidered; altered; amended; improved

____ 6. CONCLUDED F. Tapered off; became smaller or less

____ 7. MECHANISM G. To learn or possess

____ 8. ARCHIVE H. Consumed by the thought of something

____ 9. STRICT I. Small hill

____ 10. DICTATORIAL J. Branch of biology examining the relationship of organisms to one another and their environment

____ 11. RUCKUS K. List of the quantity of items contained in an area

____ 12. DISENTANGLED L. Having to do with the parts of words

____ 13. REVISED M. Without relaxation or distraction

____ 14. BATED N. Untwisted

____ 15. ACQUIRE O. False excuse

____ 16. MEDIOCRE P. Lively

____ 17. VULGAR Q. State of being semi-transparent

____ 18. SYLLABICATION R. Decided through reasoning and deliberation

____ 19. PRETEXT S. Compact and succinct

____ 20. FEEBLE T. Path a flying object takes

____ 21. TRAJECTORY U. Collection of historical documents or records

____ 22. ECOLOGY V. Lacking charm, culture, or sophistication

____ 23. CAPSULE W. Average to below average in quality

____ 24. COMPLEMENTARY X. Commotion

____ 25. TRANSLUCENCE Y. Weak

ADVANCED SHORT ANSWER UNIT TEST - *The View from Saturday*

I. Matching

____ 1. PENNY   A. Kind of prints on the wedding invitations

____ 2. NOAH   B. Grade level of the Academic Bowl team students

____ 3. IZZY   C. Arnold's owner

____ 4. DIAMONDSTEIN   D. State where Nadia's father lives

____ 5. MICHAEL   E. Portion of the North Atlantic where marine life thrives: ____ Sea

____ 6. DRAPER   F. Epiphany competes against this school on Bowl Day.

____ 7. WAGON   G. Izzy's last name

____ 8. OPERA   H. Noah used his red one to transport things to the clubhouse.

____ 9. FLORIDA   I. Master of Ceremonies at the district playoffs

____ 10. POTTER   J. Margaret's last name before marrying Izzy

____ 11. LUCAS   K. Ethan really enjoyed this performance: Phantom of the ____

____ 12. GERSHOM   L. Ginger's stage role

____ 13. SIXTH   M. Term meaning pleasingly plump

____ 14. HOVERING   N. Ham's last name

____ 15. ZATFIG   O. Dr. __: Noah's father; Nadia's mother works for him

____ 16. FAIRBAIN   P. Nadia's father's new best thing

____ 17. LETTER   Q. B & B: a kind of ____ Noah had to write

____ 18. PARAPLEGIC   R. Ethan's older, perfect brother

____ 19. SANDY   S. Best man at the wedding

____ 20. KNAPP   T. Julian magically placed one in the hand of each of The Souls.

____ 21. ROHMER   U. The Souls found this on their journey.

____ 22. MAXWELL   V. District Superintendent of Clarion County

____ 23. KINDNESS   W. Ethan or Lucas

____ 24. SARGASSO   X. Margaret's husband; Nadia's grandfather

____ 25. PAW   Y. Word describing Mrs. Olinski's physical condition

The View From Saturday Advanced Short Answer UnitTest Page 2

II. Vocabulary

    Write down the vocabulary words. Go back later and write down the correct definition for each word.

1.

2.

3.

4.

5.

6.

7.

8.

9.

10.

11.

12.

The View From Saturday Advanced Short Answer Unit Test Page 3

III. Short Answer/Quotations
Choose 10 of the following quotes and explain the importance of each to the novel. Consider our class discussions, as well as your own thoughts. Use a few sentences for each quote.

1. "To her four sixth graders puberty was something they could spell and define but had yet to experience."

2. "I concluded that many friendships are born and maintained for purely geographical reasons."

3. "Turtles had brought Grandpa and Margaret together."

4. "I did not know then that when I started sixth grade, I would be living in the state of divorce and New York."

The View From Saturday Advanced Short Answer Unit Test Page 4

5. "'Ethan Potter. I didn't recognize you.' I believe that she did not recognize him, for the person yelling *Bravo!* was Ethan, The Soul–not Ethan, the silent."

6. "He was an island unto himself, definitely not a team player. Ham Knapp was a leader. Ham Knapp had friends."

7. "Mrs. Olinski had a great tolerance for mischief, but she had no patience for malice."

8. "When people come to tea, they are courteous. She thought, I believe in courtesy. It is the way we avoid hurting people's feelings."

9. "You must know of something's existence before you can notice its absence ."

The View From Saturday Advanced Short Answer Unit Test Page 5

10. "Inside me there was a lot of best friendship that no one but Ginger was using."

11. "Like Ethan, my father has a strong taste for silence. Mother always said, 'Your father is not a communicator.'"

12. "I studied my father . . . The storm in our private lives had picked him up and put him out of place. Me, too. I, too, had been picked up from one place and set down in another. I, too, had been stranded. We both needed help resettling."

13. "'Yep,' he said. 'And there will be times when you or I will need a lift between switches.'"

14. "There is nothing wrong with Lucas, and that is what is wrong with him."

15. "Sillington House was its own place."

The View From Saturday Advanced Short Answer Unit Test Page 6

IV. Composition

Choose 2 of the following questions to discuss. Consider our class discussions, as well as your own conclusions about the novel. Be sure to cite specific examples from the novel to support your essay.

1. Do you believe that The Souls will remain friends throughout middle school and beyond? Explain, citing examples from the text to support your answer.

2. How does Margaret Draper affect the plot of the novel? Discuss her character in relation to the impact she has on the plot. Cite examples when appropriate.

3. What is the purpose of the allusions that Konigsburg uses in the novel? Choose three examples to use in your discussion.

4. Why do you think Konigsburg chose to title the novel *The View from Saturday*?

5. What role do the parents and grandparents play in this novel? Choose two of the young characters in the novel and discuss the influence their parents and/or grandparents have on them. Compare and contrast when appropriate.

ANSWER SHEET - *The View from Saturday*
Multiple Choice Unit Tests

I. Matching	II. Multiple Choice	IV. Vocabulary
1. ___	1. ___	1. ___
2. ___	2. ___	2. ___
3. ___	3. ___	3. ___
4. ___	4. ___	4. ___
5. ___	5. ___	5. ___
6. ___	6. ___	6. ___
7. ___	7. ___	7. ___
8. ___	8. ___	8. ___
9. ___	9. ___	9. ___
10. ___	10. ___	10. ___
11. ___	11. ___	11. ___
12. ___	12. ___	12. ___
13. ___	13. ___	13. ___
14. ___	14. ___	14. ___
15. ___	15. ___	15. ___
16. ___	16. ___	16. ___
17. ___	17. ___	17. ___
18. ___	18. ___	18. ___
19. ___	19. ___	19. ___
20. ___	20. ___	20. ___
	21. ___	
	22. ___	
	23. ___	
	24. ___	

ANSWER KEY - *The View from Saturday*
Multiple Choice Unit Test 1

I. Matching	II. Multiple Choice	IV. Vocabulary
1. D	1. C	1. V
2. Y	2. B	2. Y
3. K	3. D	3. U
4. R	4. A	4. X
5. C	5. B	5. L
6. L	6. B	6. D
7. T	7. C	7. F
8. S	8. B	8. H
9. M	9. C	9. G
10. I	10. C	10. N
11. N	11. D	11. J
12. B	12. A	12. W
13. W	13. C	13. B
14. F	14. D	14. A
15. O	15. C	15. P
16. U	16. B	16. R
17. A	17. B	17. S
18. V	18. B	18. M
19. G	19. C	19. K
20. E		20. O
21. P		21. I
22. H		22. T
23. Q		23. E
24. J		24. Q
25. X		25. C

ANSWER KEY - *The View from Saturday*
Multiple Choice Unit Test 2

I. Matching	II. Multiple Choice	IV. Vocabulary
1. T	1. D	1. P
2. S	2. A	2. H
3. X	3. D	3. I
4. G	4. C	4. B
5. C	5. D	5. K
6. J	6. A	6. R
7. H	7. B	7. C
8. K	8. C	8. U
9. D	9. A	9. M
10. W	10. C	10. A
11. R	11. D	11. X
12. O	12. C	12. N
13. B	13. B	13. E
14. P	14. D	14. F
15. M	15. A	15. G
16. I	16. B	16. W
17. Q	17. A	17. V
18. Y	18. D	18. L
19. L		19. O
20. N		20. Y
21. V		21. T
22. F		22. J
23. U		23. S
24. E		24. D
25. A		25. Q

UNIT RESOURCE MATERIALS

BULLETIN BOARD IDEAS - *The View from Saturday*

1. Save one corner of the board for the best of students' *The View from Saturday* writing assignments.

2. Take one of the word search puzzles from the extra activities packet and, with a marker, copy it over in a large size on the bulletin board. Write the clue words to find to one side. Invite students prior to and after class to find the words and circle them on the bulletin board.

3. Write several of the most significant quotations from the book onto the board on brightly colored paper.

4. Make a bulletin board listing the vocabulary words for this unit. As you complete sections of the novel and discuss the vocabulary for each section, write the definitions on the bulletin board. (If your board is one students face frequently, it will help them learn the words.)

5. Post the group projects related to the unit study on the bulletin board, when possible. You might also highlight pages from the unit scrapbook towards the end of the unit.

6. Post samples of calligraphy, the calligraphy alphabet, or all titles and headings in calligraphy. Also, post attempts by students to master this script.

7. Post pictures of loggerhead turtles, groups assisting loggerhead turtles, etc..

8. Post illustrations from *Alice in Wonderland* and *Through the Looking Glass* (the Tea Party, Humpty Dumpty).

9. Have students bring in photographs of themselves with their parents or grandparents. They may also bring in samples of hobbies or pictures relating to hobbies that they learned from these individuals.

10. Track an ongoing news item regarding an individual or team at your school. Post articles from various newspapers as the story or season progresses. Students may bring in articles, as well. Similarly, students may choose to create headlines based on events from the novel to post on the bulletin board.

11. Post examples of allusions from the "Allusion List," such as the Little Orphan Annie comic strip, Raphael's cherub, or playbills or representations from *Phantom of the Opera* or *Annie*.

12. Set up the bulletin board to resemble a *Jeapardy* game board. The categories could change weekly, and students could be responsible for writing the questions. Perhaps at the end of the unit, each group project topic could be a category, and the groups could write the questions relating to their topics.

Bulletin Board Ideas Continued *The View from Saturday*

13. Post a map of the United States on the board. Assign a colored string to each of the main characters, and have the class trace the journey of that character with the string. Have the students mark the places where significant events in the character's lives occurred.

EXTRA ACTIVITIES - *The View from Saturday*

One of the difficulties in teaching a novel is that all students don't read at the same speed. One student who likes to read may take the book home and finish it in a day or two. Sometimes a few students finish the in-class assignments early. The problem, then, is finding suitable extra activities for students.

One thing that seems to help is to keep a little library in the classroom. For this unit on *The View from Saturday*, you might check out the following works from the school library:

> *National Geographic Magazine*
> Collections of Mythology (including representations of Hecate)
> Art books, including the works of Raphael
> Books about etiquette
> Travel guides
> Trivia books
> *Little Orphan Annie* comics
>
> Other novels by E. L. Konigsburg, including:
> > *Jennifer, Hecate, MacBeth, William McKinley, and Me, Elizabeth*
> > *Outcasts of 19 Shuyler Place*
> > *From the Mixed-up Files of Mrs. Basil E. Frankweiler*
> > *Silent to the Bone*
> > *The Second Mrs. Gioconda*
>
> Other books that deal with subject matter in *The View from Saturday*, including:
> > *Hoot* by Carl Hiaasen (endangered species)
> > *Flush* by Carl Hiaasen (man's threat to the environment)
> > *Houdini* by Clinton Cox (biography of the famous magician)
> > *Alice in Wonderland* and *Through the Looking Glass* by Lewis Carroll

Any stories or articles about baking (especially traditional Jewish dishes), calligraphy, wedding traditions, etiquette (Emily Post, for example), ecological issues (such as endangered species), academic quiz bowl competitions, paraplegia, the Sargasso Sea, New York history and geography, magic and famous magicians, musical theater, or theatrical set design would also be of interest.

Other things you may keep on hand are puzzles. We have made some relating directly to *The View from Saturday* for you. Feel free to duplicate them for your students to use.

Some students may like to draw. You might devise a contest or allow some extra-credit grade for students who draw characters or scenes from *The View from Saturday*. This is particular appropriate for the character study portion of the unit. Note, too, that if the students do not want to keep their drawings you may pick up some extra bulletin board materials this way. If you have a contest and you supply the prize (a CD or something like that perhaps), you could, possibly, make the drawing itself a non-returnable entry fee.

The pages which follow contain games, puzzles and worksheets. The keys, when appropriate, immediately follow the puzzle or worksheet. There are two main groups of activities: one group for the unit; that is, generally relating to *The View from Saturday* text, and another group of activities related strictly to *The View from Saturday* vocabulary.

Directions for these games, puzzles and worksheets are self-explanatory. The object here is to provide you with extra materials you may use in any way you choose.

MORE ACTIVITIES - *The View from Saturday*

1. Have students work together to make a time line chronology of the events in the story. Take a large piece of construction paper and on one wall (or however you can physically arrange it in your room) and make the events of the story along it. Students may want to add drawings or cut-out pictures to represent the events (as well as a written statement).

2. Have students design a book cover (front and back and inside flaps) for *The View from Saturday*.

3. Have students design a bulletin board (ready to be put up, not just sketched) for *The View from Saturday*.

4. Have students create a chapter of the book written in the first person point-of-view by a character who does not already have a voice in the novel.

5. Have students choose one chapter of the book (with sufficient dialogue) to rewrite as a play. In conjunction with this assignment, have students write a composition explaining the difficulties they encountered in changing from one written form to another.

6. Have students take a poll of their friends, parents, grandparents, community members, etc. "The biggest single factor in the decline of Western Civilization is:" Make sure the students record the source of the claims. Have a discussion/debate on the responses, perhaps using the writing assignment they prepared in class. You might invite some of the individuals surveyed to class for the debate (invitations written by the students in calligraphy and a short tea afterwards, perhaps?)

7. Host a hobby fair. Invite members of the community, family members, and other students to set up booths and tables. Again, you can make this a small-scale affair, or a rather large one, complete with invitations, booth-headings, and thank-you notes prepared in calligraphy and a short tea following the event. Don't forget to write your B & B letters to those who donate their time and expertise!

8. Travel Log: Have students map the journeys that the characters take in the novel. Each character might be represented with a different color or a different symbol. You might keep this "map" posted throughout the unit, or you may ask each student to choose one character to map. As an accompaniment to this assignment, the students might also keep a daily travel log from the point of view of the character. At the end of the unit, they might combine all of their logs into a "scrapbook" of their journey, complete with souvenirs that they create. It would be interesting to see how individual students portray the physical and emotional journeys of the same characters differently.

9. Show any of the following:
    Alice in Wonderland (there are several versions, both animated and live)
    Annie (or play the only)
    Phantom of the Opera (or play the CD only)
    episodes of *Jeopardy* (computer and board games are also available)

10. Allow students to choose a "literature scavenger hunt" of their own, much like Julian did for his Tea Party invitations. They would have a great deal of freedom with this project, or you, as the teacher, could devise one of your own, which only becomes revealed at the end of the novel. Similarly, you might mimic Julian's technique using Carroll's novel's as a way of inviting other teachers or students to a special event.

11. Have an Activity Day- students may rotate to various stations- calligraphy (it would be useful to have a guest at this station who can teach students this skill), a turtle station, a magic station (again, a guest would be useful here), theater (with playbills, costumes, and audio/visual representations of the musical theater), a tea party. This would be a good alternative for an introduction to the unit, as well, perhaps on a day preceding Lesson 1- a good bridge between any previous unit and this one. If you choose to use a Hobby Fair as a culminating activity, this would provide a nice bridge during the introduction.

12. Have the class plan an of event to benefit or celebrate someone else. Depending on the time of year, you might host something for teachers during Teacher Appreciation Week or a celebration for students who make the honor roll or earn Student of the Week honors during the semester. Before planning the event, have your class reread the section of the novel in which the residents of Century Village meet together to contribute their time, their talents, and their coupons to the group effort of hosting the Draper/Diamondstein wedding. Similarly, you may choose to hold a drawing as part of the event–with some kind of lesson accompanying each item given away (i.e., a calligraphy set with calligraphy lessons).

WORD SEARCH The View From Saturday

```
I D I A M O N D S T E I N L Q Y J X Y T
J Z Q P Y H W R M C G L E N E T F Z T C
S J Z M U D M X J F Q A C K W R F F V M
Y L J Y L Z N M F G H N I R T A S Y Q
W W H O G L Z F X C B O K N Q S I A G L
V O N K J L L L I P M T O D C M R R Q M
W R P X S E X M E U W V R N M O B G M T
A G T E K W V Q Q P W K S E Q H A A Y H
X X X L R X W V D P H H S B S I S X T
H C T R E A T S Q Y D N A S Y R N S S D
V M Q K P M C B G M T D K M E E K O B K
Q A D N B K P I L T I Z H P T G Q Y A W
S R Y A Q H E S Z R U S A Z K O S S G H
C G S P D N R N O P A R A P L E G I C P
R A M P I S A L N U D D T I X F N X A Y
P R R S N H F W Z S L K N L L G P T L H
V E T R T C J S A W R S H M E T A H L N
C T N E O N Z C T G K C O R T S P L I S
S S N N V L U C F I O E V G T U E Q G C
V I K B Y L L D I Z M N E P E G R H R J
D N P O T T E R G N C T R D R U J N A R
L G W H Q D W N H N Q U I N L A Y R P M
K H K M V Z X V N J N R N S L T K R H N
S I L L I N G T O N N Y G G N B W K Y T
Q L E P I P H A N Y J T R O H M E R D T
```

ARNOLD	FLORIDA	LETTER	PARAPLEGIC	SINGH
AUGUST	GERSHOM	LUCAS	PAW	SIXTH
CALLIGRAPHY	GINGER	MARGARET	PENNY	SOULS
CARROLL	HAM	MAXWELL	POTTER	TREATS
CENTURY	HOVERING	MICHAEL	PUPPY	TURTLES
DIAMONDSTEIN	HYGIENIST	MONKEY	PUZZLE	VET
DRAPER	IZZY	NOAH	ROHMER	WAGON
EPIPHANY	KINDNESS	OLINSKI	SANDY	ZATFIG
ETHAN	KNAPP	OPERA	SARGASSO	
FAIRBAIN	KORSHAK	PAPER	SILLINGTON	

WORD SEARCH ANSWER KEY The View From Saturday

ARNOLD	FLORIDA	LETTER	PARAPLEGIC	SINGH
AUGUST	GERSHOM	LUCAS	PAW	SIXTH
CALLIGRAPHY	GINGER	MARGARET	PENNY	SOULS
CARROLL	HAM	MAXWELL	POTTER	TREATS
CENTURY	HOVERING	MICHAEL	PUPPY	TURTLES
DIAMONDSTEIN	HYGIENIST	MONKEY	PUZZLE	VET
DRAPER	IZZY	NOAH	ROHMER	WAGON
EPIPHANY	KINDNESS	OLINSKI	SANDY	ZATFIG
ETHAN	KNAPP	OPERA	SARGASSO	
FAIRBAIN	KORSHAK	PAPER	SILLINGTON	

CROSSWORD The View From Saturday

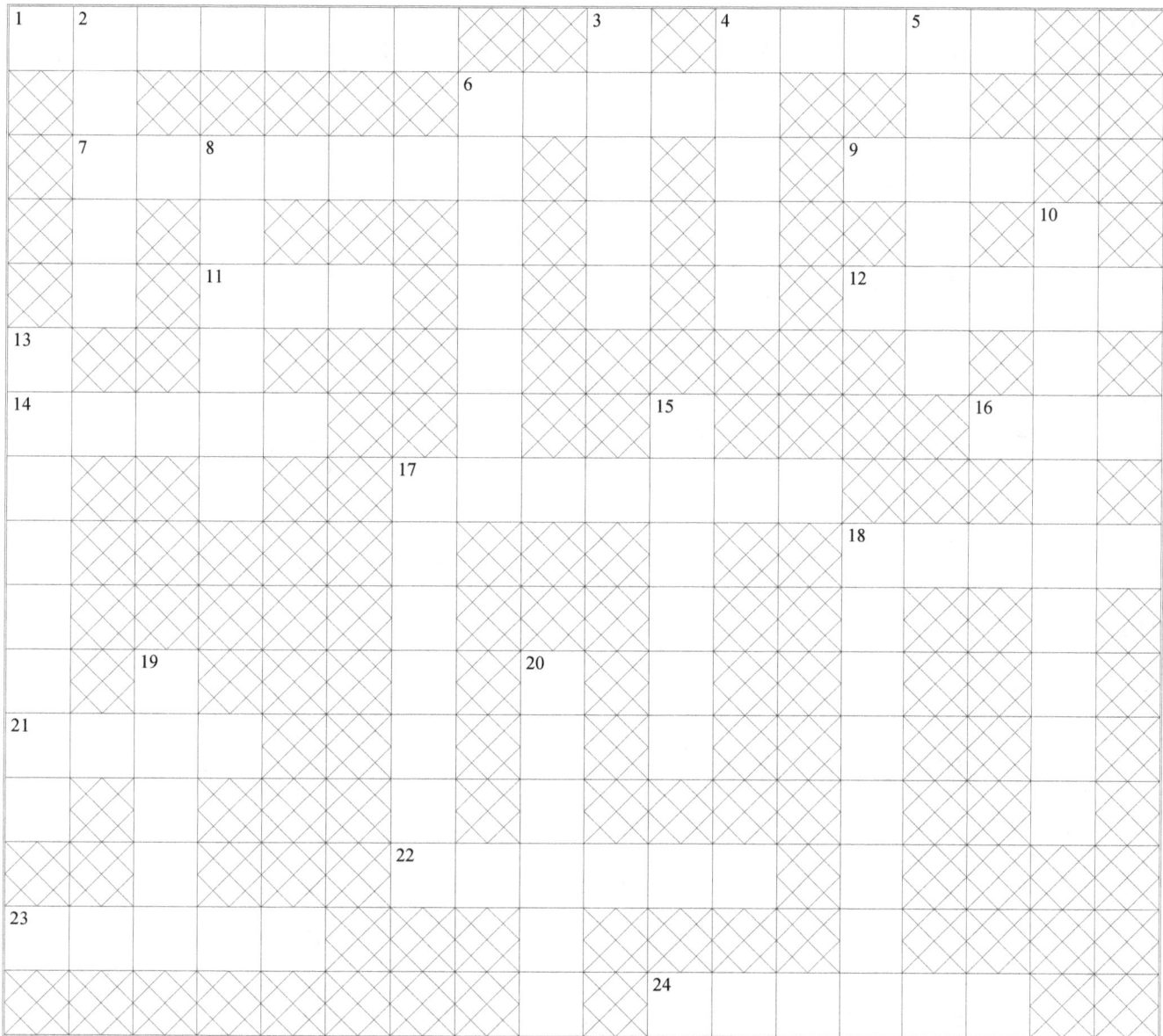

Across
1. State where Nadia's father lives
4. Grade level of the Academic Bowl team students
6. Ethan really enjoyed this performance: Phantom of the ___
7. Author of Alice in Wonderland
9. Ham's mother's occupation
11. He takes Julian's book bag.
12. Margaret's grandson
14. Nadia had the longest strip of wall ___.
16. Kind of prints on the wedding invitations
17. Arnold's owner
18. Name of the Academic Bowl team: The ___
21. Best man at the wedding
22. B & B: a kind of ___ Noah had to write
23. Julian's last name
24. Ginger's understudy

Down
2. Ethan's older, perfect brother
3. Julian magically placed one in the hand of each of The Souls.
4. Ginger's stage role
5. Ham laced Ginger's with tranquilizers and laxatives
6. She selects the Academic Bowl team members.
8. District Superintendent of Clarion County
10. Word describing Mrs. Olinski's physical condition
13. The Souls attended ___ Middle School.
15. Term meaning pleasingly plump
17. Epiphany competes against this school on Bowl Day.
18. Portion of the North Atlantic where marine life thrives: ___ Sea
19. Noah used his red one to transport things to the clubhouse.
20. Ethan or Lucas

CROSSWORD ANSWER KEY The View From Saturday

	F	L	O	R	I	D	A			P		S	I	X	T	H	
		U					O	P	E	R	A				R		
		C	A	R	R	O	L	L		N		N		V	E	T	
		A		O			I			N		D		A			P
		S		H	A	M		N		Y		Y		E	T	H	A	N
E				M				S						S			R	
P	A	P	E	R				K			Z					P	A	W
I			R			M	I	C	H	A	E	L					P	
P						A			T					S	O	U	L	S
H						X			F					A			E	
A		W						P		I				R			G	
N	O	A	H			E		O				G		G			I	
Y		G				L		T						A			C	
		O			L	E	T	T	E	R				S			
S	I	N	G	H				E						S			
							A	R	N	O	L	D					

Across
1. State where Nadia's father lives
4. Grade level of the Academic Bowl team students
6. Ethan really enjoyed this performance: Phantom of the ___
7. Author of Alice in Wonderland
9. Ham's mother's occupation
11. He takes Julian's book bag.
12. Margaret's grandson
14. Nadia had the longest strip of wall ___.
16. Kind of prints on the wedding invitations
17. Arnold's owner
18. Name of the Academic Bowl team: The ___
21. Best man at the wedding
22. B & B: a kind of ____ Noah had to write
23. Julian's last name
24. Ginger's understudy

Down
2. Ethan's older, perfect brother
3. Julian magically placed one in the hand of each of The Souls.
4. Ginger's stage role
5. Ham laced Ginger's with tranquilizers and laxatives
6. She selects the Academic Bowl team members.
8. District Superintendent of Clarion County
10. Word describing Mrs. Olinski's physical condition
13. The Souls attended ___ Middle School.
15. Term meaning pleasingly plump
17. Epiphany competes against this school on Bowl Day.
18. Portion of the North Atlantic where marine life thrives: ___ Sea
19. Noah used his red one to transport things to the clubhouse.
20. Ethan or Lucas

MATCHING 1 The View From Saturday

___ 1. PUPPY   A. The Souls attended ___ Middle School.
___ 2. GERSHOM   B. Ham's mother's occupation
___ 3. OPERA   C. Gift Ethan takes to the first tea party
___ 4. MAXWELL   D. Master of Ceremonies at the district playoffs
___ 5. CARROLL   E. Arnold's owner
___ 6. PARAPLEGIC   F. Nadia's dog
___ 7. FAIRBAIN   G. Julian's toy symbolizing balance: ivory ___
___ 8. MICHAEL   H. Julian's last name
___ 9. TURTLES   I. Author of Alice in Wonderland
___10. IZZY   J. Nadia's father's new best thing
___11. ZATFIG   K. Ginger's stage role
___12. CALLIGRAPHY   L. Noah teaches this skill to The Souls.
___13. GINGER   M. B & B: a kind of ____ Noah had to write
___14. PUZZLE   N. Nadia takes this gift to the first tea party
___15. AUGUST   O. Epiphany competes against this school on Bowl Day.
___16. LETTER   P. Ethan really enjoyed this performance: Phantom of the ___
___17. PENNY   Q. Dr. __: Noah's father; Nadia's mother works for him
___18. MONKEY   R. Name of the Academic Bowl team: The ___
___19. SOULS   S. Nadia spends this month with her father.
___20. VET   T. Term meaning pleasingly plump
___21. SANDY   U. They brought Margaret and Izzy together.
___22. HOVERING   V. Margaret's husband; Nadia's grandfather
___23. POTTER   W. Julian magically placed one in the hand of each of The Souls.
___24. EPIPHANY   X. Ethan or Lucas
___25. SINGH   Y. Word describing Mrs. Olinski's physical condition

MATCHING 1 ANSWER KEY The View From Saturday

N - 1. PUPPY	A.	The Souls attended ___ Middle School.
Q - 2. GERSHOM	B.	Ham's mother's occupation
P - 3. OPERA	C.	Gift Ethan takes to the first tea party
O - 4. MAXWELL	D.	Master of Ceremonies at the district playoffs
I - 5. CARROLL	E.	Arnold's owner
Y - 6. PARAPLEGIC	F.	Nadia's dog
D - 7. FAIRBAIN	G.	Julian's toy symbolizing balance: ivory ___
E - 8. MICHAEL	H.	Julian's last name
U - 9. TURTLES	I.	Author of Alice in Wonderland
V -10. IZZY	J.	Nadia's father's new best thing
T -11. ZATFIG	K.	Ginger's stage role
L -12. CALLIGRAPHY	L.	Noah teaches this skill to The Souls.
F -13. GINGER	M.	B & B: a kind of ___ Noah had to write
C -14. PUZZLE	N.	Nadia takes this gift to the first tea party
S -15. AUGUST	O.	Epiphany competes against this school on Bowl Day.
M -16. LETTER	P.	Ethan really enjoyed this performance: Phantom of the ___
W -17. PENNY	Q.	Dr. ___: Noah's father; Nadia's mother works for him
G -18. MONKEY	R.	Name of the Academic Bowl team: The ___
R -19. SOULS	S.	Nadia spends this month with her father.
B -20. VET	T.	Term meaning pleasingly plump
K -21. SANDY	U.	They brought Margaret and Izzy together.
J -22. HOVERING	V.	Margaret's husband; Nadia's grandfather
X -23. POTTER	W.	Julian magically placed one in the hand of each of The Souls.
A -24. EPIPHANY	X.	Ethan or Lucas
H -25. SINGH	Y.	Word describing Mrs. Olinski's physical condition

MATCHING 2 The View From Saturday

___ 1. EPIPHANY   A. Nadia had the longest strip of wall ___.
___ 2. OLINSKI   B. Best man at the wedding
___ 3. ROHMER   C. Izzy's wife; Ethan's grandmother; former principal
___ 4. FLORIDA   D. Portion of the North Atlantic where marine life thrives: ___ Sea
___ 5. AUGUST   E. Dr. __: Noah's father; Nadia's mother works for him
___ 6. PARAPLEGIC   F. Ethan really enjoyed this performance: Phantom of the ___
___ 7. OPERA   G. Julian's last name
___ 8. PAW   H. Ethan or Lucas
___ 9. SINGH   I. Term meaning pleasingly plump
___ 10. GERSHOM   J. Arnold's owner
___ 11. MICHAEL   K. Word describing Mrs. Olinski's physical condition
___ 12. IZZY   L. The Souls found this on their journey.
___ 13. SARGASSO   M. State where Nadia's father lives
___ 14. KINDNESS   N. Kind of prints on the wedding invitations
___ 15. HYGIENIST   O. Ham laced Ginger's with tranquilizers and laxatives
___ 16. NOAH   P. He takes Julian's book bag.
___ 17. PAPER   Q. The Souls attended ___ Middle School.
___ 18. ZATFIG   R. District Superintendent of Clarion County
___ 19. TREATS   S. They brought Margaret and Izzy together.
___ 20. POTTER   T. Author of Alice in Wonderland
___ 21. MARGARET   U. Nadia's mother is a dental ___.
___ 22. TURTLES   V. Margaret's husband; Nadia's grandfather
___ 23. PENNY   W. She selects the Academic Bowl team members.
___ 24. CARROLL   X. Julian magically placed one in the hand of each of The Souls.
___ 25. HAM   Y. Nadia spends this month with her father.

MATCHING 2 ANSWER KEY The View From Saturday

Q - 1. EPIPHANY	A.	Nadia had the longest strip of wall ___.
W - 2. OLINSKI	B.	Best man at the wedding
R - 3. ROHMER	C.	Izzy's wife; Ethan's grandmother; former principal
M - 4. FLORIDA	D.	Portion of the North Atlantic where marine life thrives: ___ Sea
Y - 5. AUGUST	E.	Dr. ___: Noah's father; Nadia's mother works for him
K - 6. PARAPLEGIC	F.	Ethan really enjoyed this performance: Phantom of the ___
F - 7. OPERA	G.	Julian's last name
N - 8. PAW	H.	Ethan or Lucas
G - 9. SINGH	I.	Term meaning pleasingly plump
E - 10. GERSHOM	J.	Arnold's owner
J - 11. MICHAEL	K.	Word describing Mrs. Olinski's physical condition
V - 12. IZZY	L.	The Souls found this on their journey.
D - 13. SARGASSO	M.	State where Nadia's father lives
L - 14. KINDNESS	N.	Kind of prints on the wedding invitations
U - 15. HYGIENIST	O.	Ham laced Ginger's with tranquilizers and laxatives
B - 16. NOAH	P.	He takes Julian's book bag.
A - 17. PAPER	Q.	The Souls attended ___ Middle School.
I - 18. ZATFIG	R.	District Superintendent of Clarion County
O - 19. TREATS	S.	They brought Margaret and Izzy together.
H - 20. POTTER	T.	Author of Alice in Wonderland
C - 21. MARGARET	U.	Nadia's mother is a dental ___.
S - 22. TURTLES	V.	Margaret's husband; Nadia's grandfather
X - 23. PENNY	W.	She selects the Academic Bowl team members.
T - 24. CARROLL	X.	Julian magically placed one in the hand of each of The Souls.
P - 25. HAM	Y.	Nadia spends this month with her father.

JUGGLE LETTERS The View From Saturday

1. AOREP = 1. _____
Ethan really enjoyed this performance: Phantom of the ___

2. NMEKYO = 2. _____
Julian's toy symbolizing balance: ivory ___

3. ETASRT = 3. _____
Ham laced Ginger's with tranquilizers and laxatives

4. HMA = 4. _____
He takes Julian's book bag.

5. PCAPRIAGEL = 5. _____
Word describing Mrs. Olinski's physical condition

6. PPNAK = 6. _____
Ham's last name

7. NSENSDKI = 7. _____
The Souls found this on their journey.

8. GHRALCYPAIL = 8. _____
Noah teaches this skill to The Souls.

9. SASAOGSR = 9. _____
Portion of the North Atlantic where marine life thrives: ___ Sea

10. UETLTSR =10. _____
They brought Margaret and Izzy together.

11. FATIGZ =11. _____
Term meaning pleasingly plump

12. LCMHAIE =12. _____
Arnold's owner

13. TRETEL =13. _____
B & B: a kind of ____ Noah had to write

14. IGHSN =14. _____
Julian's last name

15. IODFRLA =15. _____
State where Nadia's father lives

16. ARRPDE =16. _____
Margaret's last name before marrying Izzy

17. RPEAP =17. _____
Nadia had the longest strip of wall ___.

18. YPAEPHIN =18. _____
The Souls attended ___ Middle School.

19. ACULS =19. _____
Ethan's older, perfect brother

20. ASDNY =20. _____
Ginger's stage role

21. IBFARINA =21. _____
Master of Ceremonies at the district playoffs

22. GWANO =22. _____
Noah used his red one to transport things to the clubhouse.

23. LOINNITGLS =23. _____
Tea party location: ___ House

24. RHRMEO =24. _____
District Superintendent of Clarion County

25. LNIKIOS =25. _____
She selects the Academic Bowl team members.

26. SXIHT =26. _____
Grade level of the Academic Bowl team students

27. NTAEH =27. _____
Margaret's grandson

28. ATRMEARG =28. _____
Izzy's wife; Ethan's grandmother; former principal

29. OEHNRVIG =29. _____
Nadia's father's new best thing

30. HAON =30. _____
Best man at the wedding

31. GGNERI =31. _____
Nadia's dog

32. YZIZ =32. _____
Margaret's husband; Nadia's grandfather

33. SKOHKAR =33. _____
Bus driver for Epiphany

34. ORETTP =34. _____
Ethan or Lucas

35. DANORL =35. _____
Ginger's understudy

36. AWLXLEM =36. _____
Epiphany competes against this school on Bowl Day.

37. UPYPP =37. _____
Nadia takes this gift to the first tea party

38. WAP =38. _____
Kind of prints on the wedding invitations

39. NNYEP =39. _____
Julian magically placed one in the hand of each of The Souls.

40. VET =40. _____
Ham's mother's occupation

41. EDDMSAOINTIN =41. _____
Izzy's last name

42. SMGHERO =42. _____
Dr. __: Noah's father; Nadia's mother works for him

43. UOLSS =43. _____
Name of the Academic Bowl team: The ___

44. RCYNTUE =44. _____
Village where Margaret and Izzy live

45. LUZPEZ =45. _____
Gift Ethan takes to the first tea party

JUGGLE LETTERS ANSWER KEY The View From Saturday

1. AOREP = 1. OPERA
   Ethan really enjoyed this performance: Phantom of the ___

2. NMEKYO = 2. MONKEY
   Julian's toy symbolizing balance: ivory ___

3. ETASRT = 3. TREATS
   Ham laced Ginger's with tranquilizers and laxatives

4. HMA = 4. HAM
   He takes Julian's book bag.

5. PCAPRIAGEL = 5. PARAPLEGIC
   Word describing Mrs. Olinski's physical condition

6. PPNAK = 6. KNAPP
   Ham's last name

7. NSENSDKI = 7. KINDNESS
   The Souls found this on their journey.

8. GHRALCYPAIL = 8. CALLIGRAPHY
   Noah teaches this skill to The Souls.

9. SASAOGSR = 9. SARGASSO
   Portion of the North Atlantic where marine life thrives: ___ Sea

10. UETLTSR =10. TURTLES
    They brought Margaret and Izzy together.

11. FATIGZ =11. ZATFIG
    Term meaning pleasingly plump

12. LCMHAIE =12. MICHAEL
    Arnold's owner

13. TRETEL =13. LETTER
    B & B: a kind of ___ Noah had to write

14. IGHSN =14. SINGH
    Julian's last name

15. IODFRLA =15. FLORIDA
    State where Nadia's father lives

16. ARRPDE =16. DRAPER
   Margaret's last name before marrying Izzy

17. RPEAP =17. PAPER
   Nadia had the longest strip of wall ___.

18. YPAEPHIN =18. EPIPHANY
   The Souls attended ___ Middle School.

19. ACULS =19. LUCAS
   Ethan's older, perfect brother

20. ASDNY =20. SANDY
   Ginger's stage role

21. IBFARINA =21. FAIRBAIN
   Master of Ceremonies at the district playoffs

22. GWANO =22. WAGON
   Noah used his red one to transport things to the clubhouse.

23. LOINNITGLS =23. SILLINGTON
   Tea party location: ___ House

24. RHRMEO =24. ROHMER
   District Superintendent of Clarion County

25. LNIKIOS =25. OLINSKI
   She selects the Academic Bowl team members.

26. SXIHT =26. SIXTH
   Grade level of the Academic Bowl team students

27. NTAEH =27. ETHAN
   Margaret's grandson

28. ATRMEARG =28. MARGARET
   Izzy's wife; Ethan's grandmother; former principal

29. OEHNRVIG =29. HOVERING
   Nadia's father's new best thing

30. HAON =30. NOAH
   Best man at the wedding

31. GGNERI =31. GINGER
   Nadia's dog

32. YZIZ =32. IZZY
Margaret's husband; Nadia's grandfather

33. SKOHKAR =33. KORSHAK
Bus driver for Epiphany

34. ORETTP =34. POTTER
Ethan or Lucas

35. DANORL =35. ARNOLD
Ginger's understudy

36. AWLXLEM =36. MAXWELL
Epiphany competes against this school on Bowl Day.

37. UPYPP =37. PUPPY
Nadia takes this gift to the first tea party

38. WAP =38. PAW
Kind of prints on the wedding invitations

39. NNYEP =39. PENNY
Julian magically placed one in the hand of each of The Souls.

40. VET =40. VET
Ham's mother's occupation

41. EDDMSAOINTIN =41. DIAMONDSTEIN
Izzy's last name

42. SMGHERO =42. GERSHOM
Dr. __: Noah's father; Nadia's mother works for him

43. UOLSS =43. SOULS
Name of the Academic Bowl team: The ___

44. RCYNTUE =44. CENTURY
Village where Margaret and Izzy live

45. LUZPEZ =45. PUZZLE
Gift Ethan takes to the first tea party

The View From Saturday Word List

No.	Word	Clue/Definition
1.	ARNOLD	Ginger's understudy
2.	AUGUST	Nadia spends this month with her father.
3.	CALLIGRAPHY	Noah teaches this skill to The Souls.
4.	CARROLL	Author of Alice in Wonderland
5.	CENTURY	Village where Margaret and Izzy live
6.	DIAMONDSTEIN	Izzy's last name
7.	DRAPER	Margaret's last name before marrying Izzy
8.	EPIPHANY	The Souls attended ___ Middle School.
9.	ETHAN	Margaret's grandson
10.	FAIRBAIN	Master of Ceremonies at the district playoffs
11.	FLORIDA	State where Nadia's father lives
12.	GERSHOM	Dr. __: Noah's father; Nadia's mother works for him
13.	GINGER	Nadia's dog
14.	HAM	He takes Julian's book bag.
15.	HOVERING	Nadia's father's new best thing
16.	HYGIENIST	Nadia's mother is a dental ___.
17.	IZZY	Margaret's husband; Nadia's grandfather
18.	KINDNESS	The Souls found this on their journey.
19.	KNAPP	Ham's last name
20.	KORSHAK	Bus driver for Epiphany
21.	LETTER	B & B: a kind of _____ Noah had to write
22.	LUCAS	Ethan's older, perfect brother
23.	MARGARET	Izzy's wife; Ethan's grandmother; former principal
24.	MAXWELL	Epiphany competes against this school on Bowl Day.
25.	MICHAEL	Arnold's owner
26.	MONKEY	Julian's toy symbolizing balance: ivory ___
27.	NOAH	Best man at the wedding
28.	OLINSKI	She selects the Academic Bowl team members.
29.	OPERA	Ethan really enjoyed this performance: Phantom of the ___
30.	PAPER	Nadia had the longest strip of wall ___.
31.	PARAPLEGIC	Word describing Mrs. Olinski's physical condition
32.	PAW	Kind of prints on the wedding invitations
33.	PENNY	Julian magically placed one in the hand of each of The Souls.
34.	POTTER	Ethan or Lucas
35.	PUPPY	Nadia takes this gift to the first tea party
36.	PUZZLE	Gift Ethan takes to the first tea party
37.	ROHMER	District Superintendent of Clarion County
38.	SANDY	Ginger's stage role
39.	SARGASSO	Portion of the North Atlantic where marine life thrives: ___ Sea
40.	SILLINGTON	Tea party location: ___ House
41.	SINGH	Julian's last name
42.	SIXTH	Grade level of the Academic Bowl team students
43.	SOULS	Name of the Academic Bowl team: The ___
44.	TREATS	Ham laced Ginger's with tranquilizers and laxatives
45.	TURTLES	They brought Margaret and Izzy together.
46.	VET	Ham's mother's occupation
47.	WAGON	Noah used his red one to transport things to the clubhouse.
48.	ZATFIG	Term meaning pleasingly plump

VOCABULARY RESOURCE MATERIALS

VOCABULARY WORD SEARCH View From Saturday

```
I N A T U R A L I Z A T I O N E P M O D
N R X R E J N F M L V N C D E X R A R X
V D O A Z R I C F A V A E M G C E I I Z
E O T N E E M B Q E L S E L E T M G N
N M R S I R A I R G E I L W E S E I N Y
T I A L R C T G N C B C P C S X D N Q
O C J U F O E K R A U Q E T I T J A M
R I E C A I D A H R L J N R Y V R S T G
Y L C E C D P C O N E L L P D E P I E C
N E T N Q E E V O L L K Y E G D J N C F
Y S O C U M A D B I L Z N T B E U C O P
K J R E I F K E I V F I M U R S T U L F
C G Y K R Q E W S C A F V A D I O B O H
B Z D N E F R T H R T Z E L S V R A G P
E V I H C R A U F Q N A M D O E M T Y B
N H V C H T N E C S I T T B V R E I D N
E P E F T C R C N K A L S O E L N N E J
V R R W O C K A M V U L G A R G T G R W
O E S A M N N P U N Q S D U E I N V E G
L C I B M T O S R L S V F W I E A R V L
E E T B A B L U O J I N N J G F C L O H
N D Y R M M T L L C S U R V X N A L A H P
T E Y A B Y E E E V O S T C I R T S S C
L N R W K P J D D D H B D E F A C T O D
Y T I N E V I T A B L E P R E C E D E D
```

ACQUIRE	DIVERSITY	MAIMED	REFRAINED
ADORN	DOMICILES	MALICE	REVISED
ADVISED	ECOLOGY	MAMMOTH	RUCKUS
AMBLED	EXCESSIVE	MECHANISM	SOVEREIGN
ANIMATED	FAVORABLE	MEDIOCRE	STRICT
ARCHIVE	FEEBLE	NATURALIZATION	TERMINALLY
BATED	FRIEZE	NEGLECT	TORMENT
BENEVOLENTLY	GENUS	ORIGINATE	TRAJECTORY
BRAWN	HOVERED	PARCELED	TRANSLUCENCE
CAPSULE	INCUBATING	PERPETUAL	UNFURL
CARAFE	INEVITABLE	PHALANX	UNRULY
COIFFED	INVENTORY	PRECEDED	VERGE
DECORUM	IRONIC	PRECEDENT	VULGAR
DEFACTO	JUBILANT	PRETEXT	
DICTATORIAL	KNOLL	QUAINT	

VOCABULARY WORD SEARCH ANSWER KEY View From Saturday

ACQUIRE	DIVERSITY	MAIMED	REFRAINED
ADORN	DOMICILES	MALICE	REVISED
ADVISED	ECOLOGY	MAMMOTH	RUCKUS
AMBLED	EXCESSIVE	MECHANISM	SOVEREIGN
ANIMATED	FAVORABLE	MEDIOCRE	STRICT
ARCHIVE	FEEBLE	NATURALIZATION	TERMINALLY
BATED	FRIEZE	NEGLECT	TORMENT
BENEVOLENTLY	GENUS	ORIGINATE	TRAJECTORY
BRAWN	HOVERED	PARCELED	TRANSLUCENCE
CAPSULE	INCUBATING	PERPETUAL	UNFURL
CARAFE	INEVITABLE	PHALANX	UNRULY
COIFFED	INVENTORY	PRECEDED	VERGE
DECORUM	IRONIC	PRECEDENT	VULGAR
DEFACTO	JUBILANT	PRETEXT	
DICTATORIAL	KNOLL	QUAINT	

VOCABULARY CROSSWORD View From Saturday

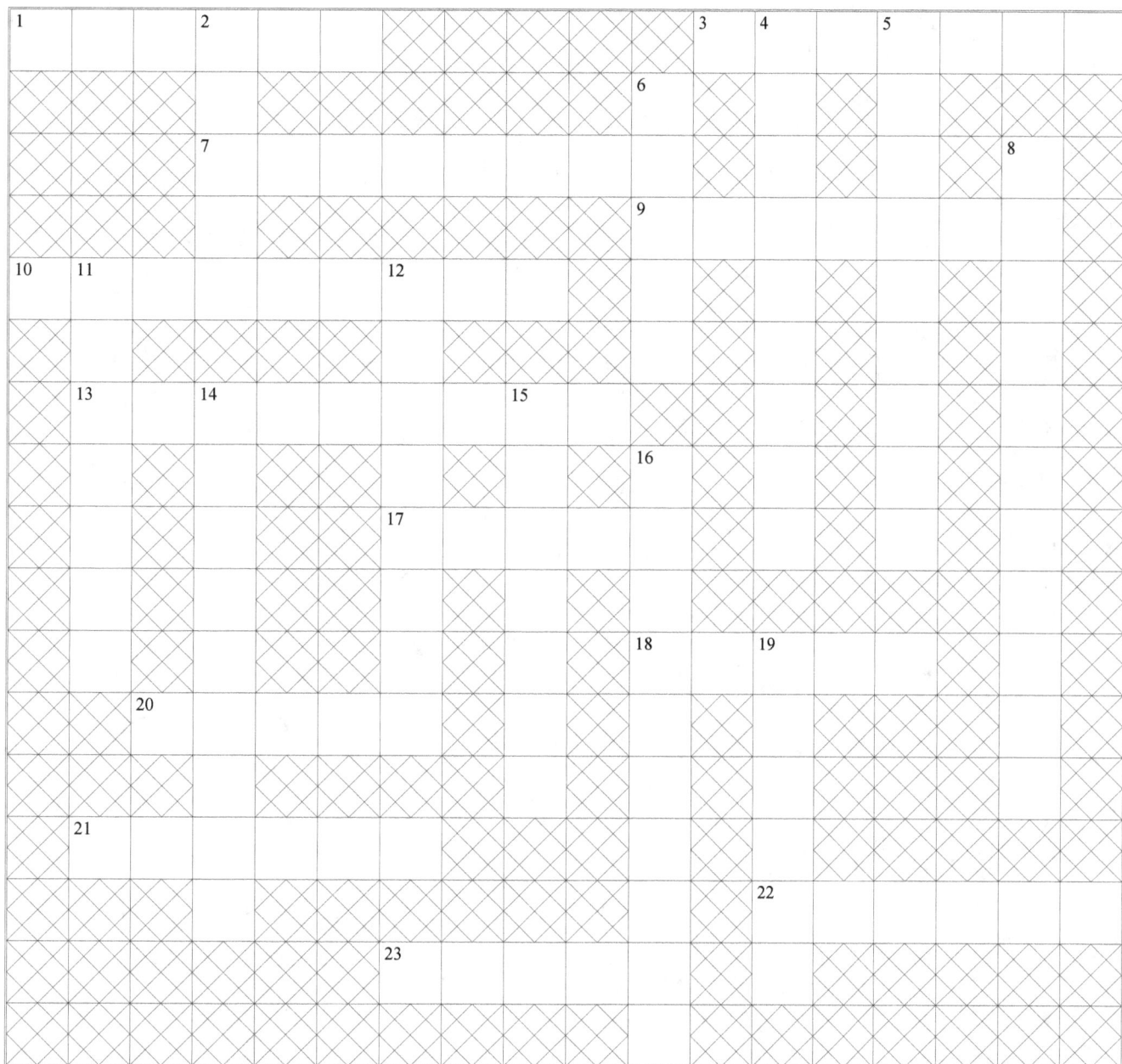

Across
1. Weak
3. Lingered without purpose
7. Precisely correct
9. Inattention
10. Traveling
13. Kept oneself from doing something
17. Decorate splendidly
18. A point or limit
20. Tapered off; became smaller or less
21. Lacking charm, culture, or sophistication
22. Hard to control
23. Small hill

Down
2. Physical strength
4. Have a beginning
5. More than is needed or wanted
6. In biology, a category above species and below family
8. Extremely badly
11. Intense suffering
12. Lively
14. Showing approval
15. Branch of biology examining the relationship of organisms to one another and their environment
16. Certain; with an unavoidable outcome
19. Commotion

VOCABULARY CROSSWORD ANSWER KEY View From Saturday

Across
1. Weak
3. Lingered without purpose
7. Precisely correct
9. Inattention
10. Traveling
13. Kept oneself from doing something
17. Decorate splendidly
18. A point or limit
20. Tapered off; became smaller or less
21. Lacking charm, culture, or sophistication
22. Hard to control
23. Small hill

Down
2. Physical strength
4. Have a beginning
5. More than is needed or wanted
6. In biology, a category above species and below family
8. Extremely badly
11. Intense suffering
12. Lively
14. Showing approval
15. Branch of biology examining the relationship of organisms to one another and their environment
16. Certain; with an unavoidable outcome
19. Commotion

VOCABULARY MATCHING 1 View From Saturday

___ 1. CONVERSION A. Divided into smaller units
___ 2. BRAWN B. Combining in such a way as to enhance each other
___ 3. FRIEZE C. Doing something against one's will
___ 4. DOMICILES D. Variety
___ 5. SPONTANEOUS E. Having to do with the parts of words
___ 6. REVISED F. In biology, a category above species and below family
___ 7. CARDINAL G. Physical strength
___ 8. INEVITABLE H. Offered advice; recommended
___ 9. STRICT I. Homes
___ 10. COMPLEMENTARY J. Fundamental
___ 11. SOVEREIGN K. King who is supreme ruler
___ 12. VULGAR L. Keeping eggs warm until hatchlings emerge
___ 13. INCUBATING M. Without relaxation or distraction
___ 14. NANOSECOND N. Certain; with an unavoidable outcome
___ 15. SYLLABICATION O. Tapered off; became smaller or less
___ 16. INVOLUNTARILY P. Something that has changed into another form, substance, state, or product
___ 17. ORIGINATE Q. A point or limit
___ 18. ADVISED R. Reconsidered; altered; amended; improved
___ 19. GENUS S. Occurring without planning or warning
___ 20. BATED T. Lacking charm, culture, or sophistication
___ 21. PARCELED U. Have a beginning
___ 22. DIVERSITY V. More than is needed or wanted
___ 23. EXCESSIVE W. Horizontal band of decoration in a building
___ 24. COIFFED X. Tiniest fraction of a second
___ 25. VERGE Y. Characterized by carefully styled, immaculate hairdo

VOCABULARY MATCHING 1 ANSWER KEY View From Saturday

P - 1.	CONVERSION	A. Divided into smaller units
G - 2.	BRAWN	B. Combining in such a way as to enhance each other
W - 3.	FRIEZE	C. Doing something against one's will
I - 4.	DOMICILES	D. Variety
S - 5.	SPONTANEOUS	E. Having to do with the parts of words
R - 6.	REVISED	F. In biology, a category above species and below family
J - 7.	CARDINAL	G. Physical strength
N - 8.	INEVITABLE	H. Offered advice; recommended
M - 9.	STRICT	I. Homes
B - 10.	COMPLEMENTARY	J. Fundamental
K - 11.	SOVEREIGN	K. King who is supreme ruler
T - 12.	VULGAR	L. Keeping eggs warm until hatchlings emerge
L - 13.	INCUBATING	M. Without relaxation or distraction
X - 14.	NANOSECOND	N. Certain; with an unavoidable outcome
E - 15.	SYLLABICATION	O. Tapered off; became smaller or less
C - 16.	INVOLUNTARILY	P. Something that has changed into another form, substance, state, or product
U - 17.	ORIGINATE	Q. A point or limit
H - 18.	ADVISED	R. Reconsidered; altered; amended; improved
F - 19.	GENUS	S. Occurring without planning or warning
O - 20.	BATED	T. Lacking charm, culture, or sophistication
A - 21.	PARCELED	U. Have a beginning
D - 22.	DIVERSITY	V. More than is needed or wanted
V - 23.	EXCESSIVE	W. Horizontal band of decoration in a building
Y - 24.	COIFFED	X. Tiniest fraction of a second
Q - 25.	VERGE	Y. Characterized by carefully styled, immaculate hairdo

VOCABULARY MATCHING 2 View From Saturday

___ 1. MEDIOCRE   A. Method or instinct an animal has for finding its way

___ 2. PROTRUDING   B. Pertaining to a variety of cultural groups

___ 3. DISENTANGLED   C. Untwisted

___ 4. NATURALIZATION   D. Irreversibly

___ 5. DECORUM   E. Came from different directions toward a central point

___ 6. ADORN   F. Sticking out

___ 7. PRECEDED   G. Average to below average in quality

___ 8. MULTICULTURALISM   H. Having to do with the parts of words

___ 9. TRANSLUCENCE   I. Decorate splendidly

___10. ACQUIRE   J. Existing in fact

___11. MECHANISM   K. Reconsidered; altered; amended; improved

___12. ITINERANT   L. Process of granting citizenship to a foreigner

___13. NEGLECT   M. To learn or possess

___14. REVISED   N. King who is supreme ruler

___15. CARAFE   O. Prevented from being expressed; kept down

___16. PERPETUAL   P. State of being semi-transparent

___17. PARCELED   Q. Continuing without change or end

___18. INCUBATING   R. Occurring in a manner opposite to what is expected

___19. SOVEREIGN   S. Inattention

___20. IRONIC   T. Traveling

___21. DEFACTO   U. Glass receptacle with an open top used for holding liquid

___22. SUPPRESSED   V. Keeping eggs warm until hatchlings emerge

___23. CONVERGED   W. Divided into smaller units

___24. TERMINALLY   X. To have gone before

___25. SYLLABICATION   Y. Etiquette; proper social behavior

VOCABULARY MATCHING 2 ANSWER KEY View From Saturday

G - 1. MEDIOCRE — A. Method or instinct an animal has for finding its way
F - 2. PROTRUDING — B. Pertaining to a variety of cultural groups
C - 3. DISENTANGLED — C. Untwisted
L - 4. NATURALIZATION — D. Irreversibly
Y - 5. DECORUM — E. Came from different directions toward a central point
I - 6. ADORN — F. Sticking out
X - 7. PRECEDED — G. Average to below average in quality
B - 8. MULTICULTURALISM — H. Having to do with the parts of words
P - 9. TRANSLUCENCE — I. Decorate splendidly
M -10. ACQUIRE — J. Existing in fact
A -11. MECHANISM — K. Reconsidered; altered; amended; improved
T -12. ITINERANT — L. Process of granting citizenship to a foreigner
S -13. NEGLECT — M. To learn or possess
K -14. REVISED — N. King who is supreme ruler
U -15. CARAFE — O. Prevented from being expressed; kept down
Q -16. PERPETUAL — P. State of being semi-transparent
W -17. PARCELED — Q. Continuing without change or end
V -18. INCUBATING — R. Occurring in a manner opposite to what is expected
N -19. SOVEREIGN — S. Inattention
R -20. IRONIC — T. Traveling
J -21. DEFACTO — U. Glass receptacle with an open top used for holding liquid
O -22. SUPPRESSED — V. Keeping eggs warm until hatchlings emerge
E -23. CONVERGED — W. Divided into smaller units
D -24. TERMINALLY — X. To have gone before
H -25. SYLLABICATION — Y. Etiquette; proper social behavior

VOCABULARY JUGGLE LETTERS 1 View From Saturday

1. UKRUSC = 1. _____
   Commotion

2. RDEDCEPE = 2. _____
   To have gone before

3. RNTTMOE = 3. _____
   Intense suffering

4. JNBAILUT = 4. _____
   Triumphantly happy

5. TATLOIIRDAC = 5. _____
   Behaving as if one has complete rule over others

6. URLAVG = 6. _____
   Lacking charm, culture, or sophistication

7. ENNDIRGER = 7. _____
   Version or translation

8. IMADNAET = 8. _____
   Lively

9. SNEELTINS = 9. _____
   Guards

10. TCEAACUR =10. _____
    Precisely correct

11. RTINATNEI =11. _____
    Traveling

12. NACARDIL =12. _____
    Fundamental

13. LEEFBE =13. _____
    Weak

14. LASTICOLNIBAY =14. _____
    Having to do with the parts of words

15. PTONIPA =15. _____
    Assign people to a certain task or job

16. UTAQNI =16. _____
Charmingly old-fashioned

17. ENPDETERC =17. _____
Previous event that serves as an example in the future

18. EODRGCNVE =18. _____
Came from different directions toward a central point

19. IEDAERRNF =19. _____
Kept oneself from doing something

20. ANTEIVEILB =20. _____
Certain; with an unavoidable outcome

21. EIQAZIURNTL =21. _____
Administer a drug that will soothe or calm

22. QCAUIRE =22. _____
To learn or possess

23. OLARABEFV =23. _____
Showing approval

24. UANCITNIGB =24. _____
Keeping eggs warm until hatchlings emerge

25. RIOCIN =25. _____
Occurring in a manner opposite to what is expected

26. SOCAIOUYRTL =26. _____
Extremely badly

27. ETRNELC =27. _____
Podium

28. OMHMATM =28. _____
Huge

29. EIRNAGOTI =29. _____
Have a beginning

30. IYSIETDRV =30. _____
Variety

31. LCEGTNE =31. _____
Inattention

32. UPCASEL =32. _____
Compact and succinct

33. WNRBA =33. _____
Physical strength

34. EESVXICES =34. _____
More than is needed or wanted

35. EESDDINGNATL =35. _____
Untwisted

36. DTAEB =36. _____
Tapered off; became smaller or less

37. NAZANRTIULOTIA =37. _____
Process of granting citizenship to a foreigner

VOCABULARY JUGGLE LETTERS 1 ANSWER KEY View From Saturday

1. UKRUSC = 1. RUCKUS
   Commotion

2. RDEDCEPE = 2. PRECEDED
   To have gone before

3. RNTTMOE = 3. TORMENT
   Intense suffering

4. JNBAILUT = 4. JUBILANT
   Triumphantly happy

5. TATLOIIRDAC = 5. DICTATORIAL
   Behaving as if one has complete rule over others

6. URLAVG = 6. VULGAR
   Lacking charm, culture, or sophistication

7. ENNDIRGER = 7. RENDERING
   Version or translation

8. IMADNAET = 8. ANIMATED
   Lively

9. SNEELTINS = 9. SENTINELS
   Guards

10. TCEAACUR =10. ACCURATE
    Precisely correct

11. RTINATNEI =11. ITINERANT
    Traveling

12. NACARDIL =12. CARDINAL
    Fundamental

13. LEEFBE =13. FEEBLE
    Weak

14. LASTICOLNIBAY =14. SYLLABICATION
    Having to do with the parts of words

15. PTONIPA =15. APPOINT
    Assign people to a certain task or job

16. UTAQNI =16. QUAINT
Charmingly old-fashioned

17. ENPDETERC =17. PRECEDENT
Previous event that serves as an example in the future

18. EODRGCNVE =18. CONVERGED
Came from different directions toward a central point

19. IEDAERRNF =19. REFRAINED
Kept oneself from doing something

20. ANTEIVEILB =20. INEVITABLE
Certain; with an unavoidable outcome

21. EIQAZIURNTL =21. TRANQUILIZE
Administer a drug that will soothe or calm

22. QCAUIRE =22. ACQUIRE
To learn or possess

23. OLARABEFV =23. FAVORABLE
Showing approval

24. UANCITNIGB =24. INCUBATING
Keeping eggs warm until hatchlings emerge

25. RIOCIN =25. IRONIC
Occurring in a manner opposite to what is expected

26. SOCAIOUYRTL =26. ATROCIOUSLY
Extremely badly

27. ETRNELC =27. LECTERN
Podium

28. OMHMATM =28. MAMMOTH
Huge

29. EIRNAGOTI =29. ORIGINATE
Have a beginning

30. IYSIETDRV =30. DIVERSITY
Variety

31. LCEGTNE =31. NEGLECT
Inattention

32. UPCASEL =32. CAPSULE
Compact and succinct

33. WNRBA =33. BRAWN
Physical strength

34. EESVXICES =34. EXCESSIVE
More than is needed or wanted

35. EESDDINGNATL =35. DISENTANGLED
Untwisted

36. DTAEB =36. BATED
Tapered off; became smaller or less

37. NAZANRTIULOTIA =37. NATURALIZATION
Process of granting citizenship to a foreigner

VOCABULARY JUGGLE LETTERS 2 View From Saturday

1. DNTRIUOPRG   = 1. _____
                        Sticking out

2. OEFIDFC   = 2. _____
                        Characterized by carefully styled, immaculate hairdo

3. EVEGR   = 3. _____
                        A point or limit

4. OMRYNCSA   = 4. _____
                        Word created from the initial letters of words in a longer phrase

5. LPAEEUTPR   = 5. _____
                        Continuing without change or end

6. LUUYNR   = 6. _____
                        Hard to control

7. UNONALYILIVTR   = 7. _____
                        Doing something against one's will

8. YDTEESNCNLNAIC   = 8. _____
                        Glowingly

9. EIZFRE   = 9. _____
                        Horizontal band of decoration in a building

10. LEEBVYOTENLN   =10. _____
                        Kindly

11. CSRTTI   =11. _____
                        Without relaxation or distraction

12. NOSDNNEOCA   =12. _____
                        Tiniest fraction of a second

13. IECRFROEN   =13. _____
                        Strengthen

14. NPOSICIER   =14. _____
                        Exact in detail

15. EFCARA   =15. _____
                        Glass receptacle with an open top used for holding liquid

16. IOCNVSOERN =16. _____
Something that has changed into another form, substance, state, or product

17. EMIMDA =17. _____
Injured permanently

18. EMIICLSOD =18. _____
Homes

19. IRUEPCEPCDO =19. _____
Consumed by the thought of something

20. TYMRECELNAOMP =20. _____
Combining in such a way as to enhance each other

21. LLNKO =21. _____
Small hill

22. NEIEFIDTLY =22. _____
Without doubt

23. ORRAECTYTJ =23. _____
Path a flying object takes

26. RUCTSCEALENN =26. _____
State of being semi-transparent

24. BLMEDA =24. _____
Strolled or walked leisurely

25. RUMDCEO =25. _____
Etiquette; proper social behavior

26. DEVNRCEOG =26. _____
Came from different directions toward a central point

27. XHAPALN =27. _____
Unit of troops who stand closely together

28. PDPSEESRUS =29. _____
Prevented from being expressed; kept down

30. CYOGLEO =30. _____
Branch of biology examining the relationship of organisms to one another and their environment

31. LNEMRALYTI =31. _____
Irreversibly

32. NTVIYREON =32. _____
List of the quantity of items contained in an area

33. ESDEVRI =33. _____
Reconsidered; altered; amended; improved

34. SCTHPATOIDISE =34. _____
Having worldly experience or culture

35. LUNRFU =35. _____
Spread out from a folded position

36. EUNSG =36. _____
In biology, a category above species and below family

VOCABULARY JUGGLE LETTERS 2 ANSWER KEY View From Saturday

1. DNTRIUOPRG = 1. PROTRUDING
Sticking out

2. OEFIDFC = 2. COIFFED
Characterized by carefully styled, immaculate hairdo

3. EVEGR = 3. VERGE
A point or limit

4. OMRYNCSA = 4. ACRONYMS
Word created from the initial letters of words in a longer phrase

5. LPAEEUTPR = 5. PERPETUAL
Continuing without change or end

6. LUUYNR = 6. UNRULY
Hard to control

7. UNONALYILIVTR = 7. INVOLUNTARILY
Doing something against one's will

8. YDTEESNCNLNAIC = 8. INCANDESCENTLY
Glowingly

9. EIZFRE = 9. FRIEZE
Horizontal band of decoration in a building

10. LEEBVYOTENLN = 10. BENEVOLENTLY
Kindly

11. CSRTTI = 11. STRICT
Without relaxation or distraction

12. NOSDNNEOCA = 12. NANOSECOND
Tiniest fraction of a second

13. IECRFROEN = 13. REINFORCE
Strengthen

14. NPOSICIER = 14. PRECISION
Exact in detail

15. EFCARA = 15. CARAFE
Glass receptacle with an open top used for holding liquid

16. IOCNVSOERN =16. CONVERSION
Something that has changed into another form, substance, state, or product

17. EMIMDA =17. MAIMED
Injured permanently

18. EMIICLSOD =18. DOMICILES
Homes

19. IRUEPCEPCDO =19. PREOCCUPIED
Consumed by the thought of something

20. TYMRECELNAOMP =20. COMPLEMENTARY
Combining in such a way as to enhance each other

21. LLNKO =21. KNOLL
Small hill

22. NEIEFIDTLY =22. DEFINITELY
Without doubt

23. ORRAECTYTJ =23. TRAJECTORY
Path a flying object takes

24. RUCTSCEALENN =24. TRANSLUCENCE
State of being semi-transparent

25. BLMEDA =25. AMBLED
Strolled or walked leisurely

26. RUMDCEO =26. DECORUM
Etiquette; proper social behavior

27. DEVNRCEOG =27. CONVERGED
Came from different directions toward a central point

28. XHAPALN =28. PHALANX
Unit of troops who stand closely together

29. PDPSEESRUS =29. SUPPRESSED
Prevented from being expressed; kept down

30. CYOGLEO =30. ECOLOGY
Branch of biology examining the relationship of organisms to one another and their environment

31. LNEMRALYTI =31. TERMINALLY
Irreversibly

32. NTVIYREON =32. INVENTORY
List of the quantity of items contained in an area

33. ESDEVRI =33. REVISED
Reconsidered; altered; amended; improved

34. SCTHPATOIDISE =34. SOPHISTICATED
Having worldly experience or culture

35. LUNRFU =35. UNFURL
Spread out from a folded position

36. EUNSG =36. GENUS
In biology, a category above species and below family

View From Saturday Vocabulary Word List

No.	Word	Clue/Definition
1.	ACCURATE	Precisely correct
2.	ACQUIRE	To learn or possess
3.	ACRONYMS	Word created from the initial letters of words in a longer phrase
4.	ADMONISH	Warn
5.	ADORN	Decorate splendidly
6.	ADVISED	Offered advice; recommended
7.	AMBLED	Strolled or walked leisurely
8.	ANIMATED	Lively
9.	APPOINT	Assign people to a certain task or job
10.	ARCHIVE	Collection of historical documents or records
11.	ATROCIOUSLY	Extremely badly
12.	BATED	Tapered off; became smaller or less
13.	BENEVOLENTLY	Kindly
14.	BRAWN	Physical strength
15.	CAPSULE	Compact and succinct
16.	CARAFE	Glass receptacle with an open top used for holding liquid
17.	CARDINAL	Fundamental
18.	COIFFED	Characterized by carefully styled, immaculate hairdo
19.	COMPLEMENTARY	Combining in such a way as to enhance each other
20.	CONCLUDED	Decided through reasoning and deliberation
21.	CONVERGED	Came from different directions toward a central point
22.	CONVERSION	Something that has changed into another form, substance, state, or product
23.	DECORUM	Etiquette; proper social behavior
24.	DEFACTO	Existing in fact
25.	DEFINITELY	Without doubt
26.	DICTATORIAL	Behaving as if one has complete rule over others
27.	DISENTANGLED	Untwisted
28.	DIVERSITY	Variety
29.	DOMICILES	Homes
30.	ECOLOGY	Branch of biology examining the relationship of organisms to one another and their environment
31.	EXCESSIVE	More than is needed or wanted
32.	FAVORABLE	Showing approval
33.	FEEBLE	Weak
34.	FRIEZE	Horizontal band of decoration in a building
35.	GENUS	In biology, a category above species and below family
36.	HOVERED	Lingered without purpose
37.	INCANDESCENTLY	Glowingly
38.	INCUBATING	Keeping eggs warm until hatchlings emerge
39.	INEVITABLE	Certain; with an unavoidable outcome
40.	INVENTORY	List of the quantity of items contained in an area
41.	INVOLUNTARILY	Doing something against one's will
42.	IRONIC	Occurring in a manner opposite to what is expected
43.	ITINERANT	Traveling
44.	JUBILANT	Triumphantly happy
45.	KNOLL	Small hill
46.	LECTERN	Podium
47.	MAIMED	Injured permanently
48.	MALICE	Wanting to do harm
49.	MAMMOTH	Huge

View From Saturday Vocabulary Word List

No.	Word	Clue/Definition
50.	MECHANISM	Method or instinct an animal has for finding its way
51.	MEDIOCRE	Average to below average in quality
52.	MULTICULTURALISM	Pertaining to a variety of cultural groups
53.	NANOSECOND	Tiniest fraction of a second
54.	NATURALIZATION	Process of granting citizenship to a foreigner
55.	NEGLECT	Inattention
56.	NONCHALANTLY	In a relaxed manner
57.	ORIGINATE	Have a beginning
58.	PARCELED	Divided into smaller units
59.	PERPETUAL	Continuing without change or end
60.	PHALANX	Unit of troops who stand closely together
61.	PRECEDED	To have gone before
62.	PRECEDENT	Previous event that serves as an example in the future
63.	PRECISION	Exact in detail
64.	PREOCCUPIED	Consumed by the thought of something
65.	PRETEXT	False excuse
66.	PROTRUDING	Sticking out
67.	QUAINT	Charmingly old-fashioned
68.	QUARTERING	Able to cut into fourths
69.	REFRAINED	Kept oneself from doing something
70.	REINFORCE	Strengthen
71.	RENDERING	Version or translation
72.	REVISED	Reconsidered; altered; amended; improved
73.	RUCKUS	Commotion
74.	SENTINELS	Guards
75.	SOPHISTICATED	Having worldly experience or culture
76.	SOVEREIGN	King who is supreme ruler
77.	SPONTANEOUS	Occurring without planning or warning
78.	STRICT	Without relaxation or distraction
79.	SUPPRESSED	Prevented from being expressed; kept down
80.	SYLLABICATION	Having to do with the parts of words
81.	TERMINALLY	Irreversibly
82.	TORMENT	Intense suffering
83.	TRAJECTORY	Path a flying object takes
84.	TRANQUILIZE	Administer a drug that will soothe or calm
85.	TRANSLUCENCE	State of being semi-transparent
86.	UNFURL	Spread out from a folded position
87.	UNRULY	Hard to control
88.	VERGE	A point or limit
89.	VULGAR	Lacking charm, culture, or sophistication

www.ingramcontent.com/pod-product-compliance
Lightning Source LLC
Chambersburg PA
CBHW051405070526
44584CB00023B/3301